ST. ANTHONY OF PADUA

Saint Anthony of Padua

LIFE OF THE WONDER-WORKER

By

ISIDORE O'BRIEN, OFM

ST. PAUL EDITIONS

Imprimi Potest:
    Fr. Mathias Faust, O.F.M.,
    Minister Provincialis.

Nihil Obstat:
    Arthur J. Scanlan, S.T.D.,
    Censor Librorum.

Imprimatur:
    ✠ Patrick Cardinal Hayes,
    Archbishop of New York.

Reprinted with the kind permission of
ST. ANTHONY'S GUILD, PATERSON, NEW JERSEY

Pictures courtesy of St. Anthony's Guild

ISBN 0-8198-0472-x c
     0-8198-0473-8 p

Printed in the U.S.A., by the Daughters of St. Paul
50 St. Paul's Ave., Jamaica Plain, Boston, MA 02130

The Daughters of St. Paul are an international congregation of women religious
serving the Church with the communications media.

Introduction

The saints are the health of our race. It is one of the chief patents of the Church's Divinity that she has always lifted up to our gaze these great figures of integrity, these heroes and heroines of the spirit who have reclaimed the human will, no matter at what cost to themselves, and so regained perfect liberty. Nor does the office of the saints stop with mere proof and example. The charity of Christ is their native air. Their first and most immediate relation to us is that they love us, in their measure, as He does in His. In the Catholic saint there is no mere pattern, noble but aloof and chill. There is the tender elder brother or sister, guiding our weakness and anticipating our needs with the same warm, selfless affection that makes family life at its best a real sacrament.

Father Isidore truly says, in the extraordinarily human and vivid interpretation that follows, that no saint in the entire calendar embodies more clearly this watchful love than does Anthony, the Wonder-worker of Padua. And never has our stricken race more sorely needed what Anthony of Padua has to give. For the wonders of

Anthony are not mere unrelated portents. He is not the mere wonder-worker — if one may put the negation without ingratitude or irreverence. He stands at the center of that Christlike thing, the Franciscan ideal. It was the most important force in his life, transforming and intensifying that life, blameless as it was, and directing his every action and impulse from the moment he felt the touch of Francis on his heart until the moment of his birth into eternity. And it is also — as we know with certainty — the only force that can save our imperiled society. Whatever may be the technical and economic factors responsible for the fearful plight of the world today, the moral factor was greed, and it was the most powerful of all. No honest thinker, Christian or pagan, denies this. And as it was greed which produced the crisis, it is, by an inexorable law, the reverse of greed which must undo the mischief, and restore justice and security. Until poverty is realized once more as the highest social ideal, gladly embraced once more because it is the thing that makes us one with Christ, material reforms will accomplish little.

The Holy See has always granted a special, if unofficial, primacy to the children of Francis, which is token enough to Catholics that the ideals of Francis have a special spiritual authority. But it is interesting that contemporary Popes have stressed this in an unmistakable manner. The great Pontiff Leo XIII anticipated the present situation, and among the many means by which he strove to avert it, his recommendation of the spread of the Third Order was the most significant. The present Holy Father, among the many memorable utterances that make us proud to be his spiritual children, has spoken a most moving endorsement of Christlike poverty, modified as may be necessary for individual circumstances, as heaven's sure remedy for our present maladies.

And what we prize in the traditional Franciscan approach is the winning grace with which this ideal is presented to us. It is not the harshness of abnegation that we learn from Christ; it is rather that the yoke is sweet and the burden light; nor do we learn it from Francis, who devised a new virtue for his followers — a joyous courtesy; nor do we learn it from Anthony the Wonderworker. It is his method to win us from inordinate devotion to material things by a meticulous recognition of real material needs. This is a logical and necessary part of Franciscanism — to control and moderate possession by sanctifying it — and it is Anthony who exemplifies it to thousands of imaginations. It is Anthony, who owns nothing and wants nothing, who baptizes our little ownings, as it were, and blesses our little wants, by taking them under his protection. Father Isidore tells us, in a most attractive passage, that only true greatness can stoop like this without losing stature, and draws the just parallel between Anthony's care of us and Mary's intervention at the wedding feast of Cana. If Mary and her Son instruct us all, by that miracle, in delicacy and promptness of imagination, regard for another's dignity, graciousness about small needs, Anthony must indeed be considered Their best pupil.

This book has a freshness of approach, an intimate and charming style, that give it a special value in a field where these literary virtues are not too plentiful. But even beyond these, it has the value of leading us to see Anthony in this light of the interpreter, the bridge-builder, who uses both his natural gifts and his supernatural prerogatives to communicate to men, in so far as they can receive it, the ideal that is all in all to him. We see him, in these pages, turning the forces of one of the great minds of the thirteenth century to no form of self-glorification, but to translate, defend and spread the simplicities of his father Francis, which were the simplicities of Christ. And we are irresistibly impelled to draw the parallel ourselves, and see him today using such a store of graces and favors as has been granted to few of the other inhabitants of heaven, not to indulge us, not even to prove the power of a Saint of God, but to win us back to those same simplicities, without which we must surely perish.

M. K.

Contents

15

1

The Setting

PRECURSORY of mien, stark of virtue, fiery of eloquence, Peter the Hermit, a holy man of Amiens, rode a donkey through Italy and southern France, and preached a mission. Men and women threw down their baskets in the vineyards and orange-groves along the slopes of the Pyrenees, and gathered round him: in awe, at first; then in indignation; and finally in a consuming enthusiasm for the cause which he preached. In the towns along the Rhone, the weaver threw aside his shuttle, the blacksmith his hammer, the carpenter his plane, and flocked to the market-place, the church and the guild-hall, to hear him, and to discuss the things of which he spoke.

From town to town rode Peter, preaching one sermon, asserting one issue — the recapture of the Saviour's Tomb from the Turks. With one cry continuously on his lips, he went through vineyard and field and wood, and the mountains resounded the echo, "God wills it!" He called on all — young and old, men and women — to deny themselves; to take up their cross; to leave all and win

Christ through pilgrimage, sacrifice and, if necessary, martyrdom. This was in the year 1095.

History furnished Peter the text. Ever since the Empress Helena, Constantine's mother, had erected a church on the hallowed spot where the True Cross was discovered, pilgrims had been going to the Holy Land in increasing throngs. On their return, they had fired the general imagination by their vivid accounts of places and people known to the masses heretofore only from the pages of the Bible. They had graphically reported, too, the mounting insolence of the Mohammedan, and the increasing difficulty of pilgrimages. The Tomb of the Saviour had, indeed, been in the hands of the infidel since the year 637, when Omar the Caliph had taken it from the Faithful. But now darker clouds were banking: Christians were being tortured and butchered — insolence had flamed into persecution. Had not the hour struck for every man and woman to help in wresting the holy places from infidel hands, and restoring security to the Christian world? It must be now or never.

At the beginning of the century, Pope Sylvester II had vainly urged their great-grandfathers to rise up and reclaim Palestine. With fresh reason, Pope Gregory VII, two generations later, had besought their fathers. And now, when through these vineyards and orange-groves was ringing the news that, of the seven thousand pil-

grims gone to Palestine with Siegfried, Archbishop of
Mainz, two-thirds had been slain, or had died of privation and ill-treatment, Pope Urban II was proclaiming
anew the imperative duty of winning back the Holy Land;
and Peter the Hermit was his mouthpiece.

The mission of Peter was not in vain. Men became
eager to throw away their plows and baskets and tools,
to take up the sword, to pin the flaming cross of silk
on their shoulders, to set out for Asia Minor, to gain
indulgences for their deed, and to win perhaps the martyr's crown.

Events marched swiftly; and, on the very eve of the
next (the twelfth) century, the crusaders took Jerusalem.
With a cross on his naked shoulder, Godfrey of Bouillon
entered the Holy City, the first Frankish King of Jerusalem. Eventually, England and Germany contributed
leaders to the crusades; but we are to remember that,
primarily, they were a Gaulish movement.

And it is likewise necessary to remember that, through
all this period, there were two distinct worlds, each held
together and interwoven by its own utterly different religious belief — a belief that made national boundaries,
though mere streams in themselves, as wide in significance
as the Atlantic Ocean. There was the world of Christ
and the world of Mohammed; the world of the Gospel
and that of the Koran. Europe, Spain excepted, was

Christian; the rest of the world, from the Pyrenees to the Himalayas, was Mohammedan.

So ran the important lines on the map in the twelfth century. One wave of crusade followed another, and boiled and broke on the Mohammedan shore. The full tide of Christian thought flowed toward Palestine. Men and women, and even little children, dreamed of glorious deeds of valor on foreign sands, of heroic acts that would bring death and deathless honor. Self-forgetfulness, loyalty to Christ, His teaching, His country, and especially those places made sacred by His physical presence as Man on earth, rose to a mystic exaltation unique in Christian history, and scarcely imaginable to a more cautious and prosaic age. For a century, mediaeval chivalry had been going through a process of religious consecration, so that now all the virtues of knighthood — faith, courtesy, gallantry, courage, honor — were symbolized in that flaming cross of red silk worn on the right shoulder: the insignia of the crusader and the banner of Godfrey of Bouillon, ancestor of Saint Anthony of Padua.

When, after the first triumphs, the news of Saint Bernard's failure reached home, one hundred thousand Germans rushed immediately into battle-line, and the armies of England and France, under Richard the Lion-hearted and Philip II, joined them. These events fell between the years 1189 and 1192. Great companies and fleets of this crusade stopped in Lisbon, where several of the English priests remained. They could not know that later there would sit at their feet a saint — a boy in quest of learning.

Thus swung a cycle of highly-colored events; a cycle through every year and month of which men's and women's minds glowed with religious fervor. Old men spoke of the First Crusade as our grandfathers talk of Gettysburg. Men of middle age spoke of the Second Crusade as our elder brothers talk of Verdun.

And it was at the end of this century of heroism; in the newly established kingdom of Portugal, itself born of a crusade; in Lisbon, a city which crusaders had set free — it was in these circumstances that Saint Anthony of Padua was born, on the Feast of Our Lady's Assumption, August 15, 1195. The blood of crusaders flowed strongly in his veins. The virtues that glorified them were baked into his very bones. The stories that men brought back from Palestine were the adventures and legends that enthralled his boyish heart. He yearned, as all boys do, to go forth, when his time should come, and meet monsters and slay dragons and endure trials and win the crown.

If, then, we later see him setting his face toward the land of the infidel, see him covering his body with a hairshirt, hear him preaching Christ Crucified, see him fasting on a mountain-top, we shall know that he is but following the ideal flung into the blue sky of Italy by Peter the Hermit, caught by Godfrey of Bouillon, carried on by Saint Bernard of Clairvaux, flashed through the length and breadth of Europe, pointed out to Anthony's infant eyes by his mother, and explained to him by the crusader priests who instructed him in his early years.

Thus walked Saint Anthony onto a stage whose properties were painted in strong colors. He was the scion of a family that had made and lived drama. Before him rose and curved a concave of breathing, muttering, shuffling, expectant darkness. The spotlight of divine grace picked him out; and within its white arc his figure stood youthful and erect.

2

The Rôle

BIOGRAPHERS of the saints generally sculpture their subjects in such heroic size that ordinary men and women are dwarfed by contrast into heartless insignificance. In their very zeal they run the risk of defeating the end of their work. They hammer us into insensibility by relentless laudation, by hurling at us every possible fact or fancy in the life of their saint that makes him stand out as utterly different from the rest of mankind.

What we must remember, always, is that Saint Anthony was not born a saint, but an infant subject to human frailty even as we. He was a mortal creature meeting temptations, having days of dryness and loneliness, like every other son of Adam. He differed from us in this, that he "made with temptation issue". It is just this possibility of sin and actuality of virtue; this close resemblance to us in trial and difference in triumph; this daily struggle in the details of his inner life, that makes Saint Anthony so valuable a model, and which most of his biographers have omitted. He was a blade of grass in the greensward of common humanity; but temptation could not scorch him. Frost and darkness had no power to wither or destroy him.

Saint Anthony's biographers lay great stress on the fact that his mother dedicated him at baptism to the Blessed Virgin. There can be no holier practice, surely. Yet we must remember that during the last two thousand years, a hundred million mothers have done this very thing. Your mother and mine probably dedicated us to God and Mary in thought and word a hundred times; nevertheless we are noticeably different still from Saint Anthony. He was born near a church, they tell us; yet few of us were born in the wilderness of pagan lands. We know the church of our childhood as well as we know our mother's face; yet we have not raised one dead person to life. Saint Anthony was taught by priests, we are told; yet a great percentage of us, too, were taught by Sisters, or Brothers, or priests; and we are all still very far from manifesting the sanctity that works miracles.

This, we know, is a human observation which we cannot push too far without danger. The point we are making from it is this: Saint Anthony, to all these holy and reverent appointments, added his own efforts toward the fulfilment of those dreams that his mother and teachers had regarding him. God gave this boy an abundance of

grace, for He cannot be outdone in generosity. If we are
not more like Saint Anthony, the fault is ours, the praise
is Saint Anthony's.

The most that our parents and teachers can do for
us is, to start us by instruction and example in the path
of manly, upright, Christian virtue, and then pray for us.
We must travel that path alone, assisted by God's grace
and guidance. This is exactly what Saint Anthony did.
He brought to quick ripening the seeds of holiness that
his mother had planted in him. From the dawn of reason he turned eagerly to God and His Blessed Mother.
It was a beautiful thing for the angels to see when Doña
Teresa dedicated her son in the temple to Mary Immaculate; it was a more glorious scene on which the
heavenly court gazed when, at the age of five, that same
son, in the presence of his fair, holy young mother, and
valiant, noble young father, dedicated his virginal purity
to Mary Immaculate. It was a beautiful sight for all
when the young boy who, at birth, had been named
Ferdinand, and whom the world would know as Saint
Anthony, served his uncle's Mass in the Cathedral of
Lisbon; yet it was a surer indication of Saint Anthony's
holiness when he traced the Cross on the altar steps to
banish a temptation of Satan's. For many boys have
served Mass in spotless surplices, have moved like angels
amid the flowers and incense and candlelight, but not

all of them in later life have consistently met the tempter's subtle suggestions with the Sign of the Cross.

Saint Anthony's early years, we read, were spent in the shadow of a church dedicated to the Blessed Virgin; and his later life, we know, was lived under the safe protection of Mary's blue mantle. Here he instructs us again; for it is to Mary we must go, and with Mary we must stay, if we are to live pure and holy lives. This was so in the twelfth century, and in the first, and is so in the twentieth. She instructed Saint Anthony, she tended Christ; she will guide and help us. Throughout Saint Anthony's life, and especially in his sermons, it was the love of Christ which Mary had taught him that feathered the arrows of his words and sped them with precision to wound the heart of sinner and heretic.

His social status brought him into easy contact with luxury and court life — two things non-conducive to heroic virtue. His father was Governor of Lisbon, the child would naturally be petted and pampered for many reasons, political and otherwise; for the surest way, then as now, to a parent's heart was by way of noticing his child. Pride and rudeness and the loss of friends have developed very frequently from this political root, but Saint Anthony passed through these temptations successfully. He made visits to Mary and the Blessed Sacrament in preference to spending his time where he would be pampered and flattered. At a very early age he saw the true relationship of so-called human greatness to the greatness of God's kingdom. "O world," he cried in his early disillusionment, "how burdensome thou art become to me! Thy power is but that of a fragile reed, thy riches are as a puff of smoke, and thy pleasures like a treacherous rock whereon virtue is shipwrecked."

In 1210, at the age of fifteen, Saint Anthony entered the Augustinian House of Studies. The college stood on the outskirts of Lisbon, and was known as St. Vincent's Outside the Walls. This building was closely connected with the settling in Lisbon of Saint Anthony's own family; for St. Vincent's had been founded by Alfonso I during the siege of Lisbon, in which Saint Anthony's grandfather distinguished himself. The king's motive in building this house was to provide a place for pilgrimages; and the motive of the pilgrimages was visits, vigils and prayers for the success of all crusaders. So even here, Saint Anthony was still breathing the very air of devotion to a great idea; was gazing, as he sat in his cell, on walls which enthusiasm for a great issue had built. St. Vincent's received its supply of priests from the Augustinian Mother-house in Coimbra — the monastery to which Saint Anthony had himself transferred two years later.

By entering this community of the Canons Regular of

St. Augustine he signified his intention of becoming a priest, and thus renounced all claims to his father's title and estates.   We know that he never turned aside from his purpose; and though we possess neither the exact date nor the circumstances of his ordination, we do know that he became a priest, though the humble offices he took upon himself in the community often led people to think him a lay Brother.   He remained with the Canons Regular of St. Augustine for ten years — two years of which he spent at St. Vincent's Monastery and eight at the Monastery of the Holy Cross in Coimbra.   The reason given for the transfer is that he wished to avoid the number of persons who still insisted on seeing and flattering him, thus taking up his time to their own advantage.   Records say that he was an exemplary student both in discipline and study.

And this is the slender sheaf of facts that research has gleaned from the rich field of the young manhood of Ferdinand Martini, or Saint Anthony of Padua, as we shall call him.

3

The Franciscan Door

"DEAREST Brothers, gladly should I take the habit of your Order *if you would promise that as soon as I do so you would send me to the land of the Saracens,* there to reap the same reward as your holy martyrs and gain a share in their glory."

These words give us expressly the condition which Ferdinand, the Augustinian Canon Regular, laid down to the emaciated mendicants who sought bread at the gates of Holy Cross — the condition governing his proposed entry into their community. With no ordinary joy the Brothers accepted this condition. And thus the door that led into the Franciscan Order and future greatness was opened to Saint Anthony. As soon as he could gain the necessary permission from the Prior and his advisers, Saint Anthony took off the white habit of Saint Augustine and put on the brown robe of Saint Francis. The exchange quite naïvely took place in the Monastery of Holy Cross itself.

The scene of this reception had its lights and shadows of human feeling; for sorrow sat on the faces of these learned and holy men among whom Ferdinand had grown up and who had guided his mind and heart in study and in religious training. These priests loved him, and it was not without human sorrow at losing the sweet-tempered companion, a sorrow probably mixed with foreboding for his future, that they took back the white habit from his hands and watched him put on the brown robe of these strange beggars. But if there was sorrow on the faces of the Augustinians, there was joy in the eyes of the Franciscans; for were they not gaining a new member, one versed in the Scriptures and trained in the scientific lore of his day? Were they not taking back with them to their humble hut one who already had, in a marked degree, the very spirit of their founder, namely, an unquenchable thirst for martyrdom and a longing to set out for the land of the infidel? Their new recruit returned with the Franciscans to their house in the olive-grove a mile from Coimbra; and as he entered his future home, he laid aside the name which had been given him at baptism, and took for his new name that of the Saint to whom this Franciscan House was dedicated. Henceforth he was called Anthony, for the little convent was known as St. Anthony's of Olivares, from the olive trees that shaded it.

Saint Anthony made this change in the summer of 1220. It was the culmination of a long line of thought, aspiration, ambition. Several incidents in the last few months had hastened the decision; and the sight of the relics of the five Franciscan martyrs of Morocco, relics that had rested beneath his eyes in the Monastery of Holy Cross, had brought the matter to quicker issue. He had spoken with these five men on their outward journey as they went to convert the Moors. Some time afterward he knelt at their tomb. He had heard the story of their martyrdom from the Brothers who came begging to the door. He had seen their bodies brought back in royal splendor; and his own thoughts were fired by the deeds of these brave men and by the glorious crown they had won. The call of his ancestors was knocking at his heart; the urge of the crusader blood was driving quickly through his veins. The battle-cry of that great century was ringing in his ears: "God wills it!" To meet the Mohammedan, for the sake of Christ; to pour out his red life-stream on the sands of Saracen territory; to be a crusader, a martyr; to be one at last with the brave men of whom he had heard such glorious and soul-stirring tales since the days of his infancy — this was the dream, the ambition, that stirred so insistently beneath the white habit of the Augustinian scholar and recluse.

The historic incidents of the previous decade had helped to crystallize this ideal. He had naturally followed the vicissitudes of contemporary Moorish warfare, especially in the Peninsula itself. He knew of the defeat of Mohammed En-Nasir at Toulouse, in 1212, of the struggle of James the Conqueror to join Moslem Valencia to Aragon. Probably with some hope for the papal cause and the promised Fifth Crusade, he had learned of the crowning at Aix-la-Chapelle of the young, progressive Emperor, Frederick II, and had rejoiced at Otto's confinement to Brunswick. He would know that Honorius III had recently written to Abu Jacob, the Miramolin, demanding better treatment for the Christians in Morocco.

Saint Anthony would be well aware of these things, and he probably knew many more secret activities that history does not record; for he was related by blood to men on the inside of the government, and we know that his acquaintances came often enough to see him. Their talk must have been mainly of the crusades and the rise and fall of Moorish activities. Besides, it would have been practically impossible for a student to live in that period and in that place and not be interested in the cause of Christ against the Mohammedans; especially for one whose secret aspiration it was to be on the battlefield himself.

Many of us have yearned ardently to throw ourselves into some undertaking, to branch out into new activities, to grasp, ere they slipped away forever, opportunities for doing mighty things for God and man. We have remained awake at night turning the project over in our tortured soul, and we have dropped off into fitful sleep at last with the question, But how? echoing through the cavern of our mind. And how was Saint Anthony to follow his dreams, go to infidel lands, become a martyr?

A man in Umbria answered the question. A cloth merchant's son in a hill town in the Italian province of that name happened at that particular time to be putting on his own personal drive against the Moors. Francis Bernardone of Assisi had made, a few years earlier, the startling discovery that if you want anything done you must do it yourself. Acting on this new-found wisdom, he had immediately discovered that he was being rated as a fool in general, and by his own father in particular, for doing the very things on whose fulfilment he had set his heart. But he was not deterred. And as it happened, among the many projects on which Francis of Assisi had set his heart, the winning of Mohammedan Asia was almost first.

About the year 1209, this Francis had progressed so far in his new mode of life that he was an accepted item of daily conversation. He drew the honest criticism of some, the cynicism of others, the love of many, the loyalty of a few; the wonder of all. He preached a strange doctrine, or one so little practised that it seemed strange. He went back to Christ and to Apostolic times for his standard of living. He prayed and wept and fasted and dreamed much. He carried stones in the burning sun to repair a crumbling church. He swept out sanctuaries with a broom. He dressed lepers with his own hands and kissed their wounds. He looked on the crucifix and his soul sank within him in love and pity. And because he dreamed much, he attempted much. By 1209, twelve companions had joined him. His fame spread.

In 1210, the year Anthony joined the Canons Regular, Francis set out for Rome. Pope Innocent III, in a strange dream one night, beheld the figure of a beggar supporting, with his sole unaided strength, the Basilica of St. John Lateran. The very next day Francis presented to the Pope a Rule of life containing twenty-three chapters which he had written as a guide for himself and his companions. This Rule was so primitive in its aspirations, and went so directly to the imitation of Christ's life, and to the practice of the virtues Christ counseled and stressed, that it caused great comment in the Papal Court. Innocent III approved it *viva voce,* and Francis returned home.

In a few years his followers numbered thousands, and were scattered in their apostolate through the villages and towns of Europe and the Islands— a clear proof that other men had been dreaming of doing great things for God and man, and were but awaiting the saint and genius who should open the door to their knockings; should show them the armor to wear and the road to travel in the accomplishment of their long-nurtured designs.

As we have said, the conquest of Mohammedans, Saracens and Moors was a pet project of Francis. But with characteristic genius he had shifted the mark toward which his own and his followers' endeavors must be directed. From Godfrey of Bouillon down, all the hermits, crusaders and saints had striven to wrest from the Mohammedan lands, cities and sacred places for the glory and service of Christ. Francis, with one quick step, went beyond all their highest ambitions: he set out to wrest the Mohammedan from himself for the glory and service of Christ. It was this inspiration of his that opened the door to Saint Anthony's ambition, and made it possible to unite the dream of the crusader with the prayer of the recluse.

Saint Francis was never content with dreaming a beautiful dream; action always quickly followed. And so in the year 1213, we find him setting out single-handed to bring back to Christ, not the land of Africa, but the people of Africa. He actually got as far west in this march on Africa as the Peninsula, when sickness fell on him and forced him to return. And though he had failed in his major project, he had grasped one thing clearly, namely, the possibility of this route through the west to Mohammedan territory, a route roundabout, but clear and safe for Christian travel. It lay through Aragon and Castile, across Portugal to Lisbon, and thus to the open sea.

This discovery made by Saint Francis has a most direct bearing on this story; for since his own endeavors in 1213 had failed, in 1217 he sent eight of his companions by this route on the errand of conquest. Two of these were destined to remain in Portugal; their names were Walter and Zachary, and they made their way finally into Coimbra. Sancia, the king's sister, gave them one house near Alenquer; the queen gave them another within a mile of Coimbra, which later was St. Anthony's of Olivares. These houses were outposts of the expedition; and it was by this route, and stopping for final refreshment and rest at these houses, that the followers of Saint Francis determined to advance on Africa. It was thus the five martyrs of Morocco came to Coimbra; and it was because the Franciscans lived by alms, and because they often solicited them at the door of the Augustinian Monastery of Holy Cross, to which Saint Anthony attended in the rôle of guest-master, that he learned eventually of these dreamers, crusaders, aspirants to martyrdom, learned of these men whose thoughts ran so closely parallel to his own.

Saint Francis, of course, defies all analysis. He is a saint, and then something more than a saint. He is the high-priest of naturalists, and then something beyond that. He is the great humanitarian and philanthropist, and then something greater than these. And this extra imponderable measure is a love unbounded, uncharterable. He came and threw open the windows and let into men's lives the sunshine and the fresh morning air, the perfume of a thousand wild flowers of sympathy and love, the rippling sound of tumbling brooks, that was prayer ever rising to the heart of God. He inspired men to heroic things, for his sunny presence banished from their minds the miasmic vapors of selfishness and greed and impurity. Saint Francis came and touched all things to gladder life. And the gladdest transformation he wrought was when his voice, coming across the hills of Italy, and ringing down the valleys of Portugal, called the young Augustinian Canon from an immortal dream to the glorious adventure of its realization.

4

The Martyrdom
of Failure

SAINT ANTHONY, with a companion, left Coimbra in 1220. He sailed from Lisbon down the coast to Morocco. No sooner had he landed than he caught a fever which held him prostrate for several months in Africa. When strong enough to travel, he set out for home. Of that journey we shall speak in a moment. Here we note that during his stay in Morocco he did not preach one sermon, convert one Moor, lose one drop of blood at Saracen hands: he simply went to Africa, took sick, remained there until someone nursed him back to health, and left again.

Thus ended the story of Saint Anthony as a crusader. It is short, for it never takes long to recount a failure. However, if it had not ended thus, this story of ours would never have been written.

Saint Anthony, like many of us, failed in the very project on which he had set his heart most definitely. And saint though he is, kind and tender and helpful though he has been, if Anthony had never failed in anything he attempted, he would be without that human touch which endears him to those men and women who have played their part so nobly and on whose defeat the curtain has rung down. He would then be less like men and very much less like the God-man. Saint Anthony has sympathized with us a hundred times, but in this one instance we sympathize with him: we give him the silent handclasp of perfect understanding, an understanding that only failure, forced on us before the watching eyes of all, can bring to life in us.

Generally speaking, he was a success. He was first in his classes in the Augustinian House of Studies. At Holy Cross he was looked upon as a brilliant theologian. His opinions had a high standard of merit compared even with those of distinguished doctors from Paris. He had succeeded in making two changes in his religious life which probably not another young Augustinian religious in Lisbon or Coimbra could have effected. Later, he was the greatest preacher of his day. He was called "The Hammer of Heretics", "The Ark of the Covenant"; he was selected by Saint Francis to train Franciscan minds.

Yet notwithstanding all these triumphs, the ambition nearest and dearest to his generous heart ended in dismal failure. He had thought much regarding it before he made any move to change his life; he had prayed and meditated, worked and sought counsel; and it had seemed to him that his life's labors lay among the

Saracens. With the blessing of his superiors on his head, and the glory of God before his eyes, he had stood one day in the late fall by the ship's rail, watching the high foreland of Portugal sink into the blurred background of evening. He had watched the prow of the vessel rise and fall as she plowed through the broken waves of the Atlantic; his face had lighted with the eagerness of young manhood and the whole-souled ambition for martyrdom, as he had awakened one morning to see the breakers tumbling white in a froth-line upon the African shore. This triumph was short-lived. The first hot breath from that dark mysterious land had laid low forever his chances for a martyr's death. A martyr of desire he surely is, as Saint Bonaventure so beautifully says. But with desire his martyrdom ended. Through long weeks of pallid inactivity he lay and reviewed this adventure on which he had started with such high promise. Those around him suggested that he return home. He fought at first against the idea; but as the days dragged on and his form wasted away with fever, he gave up the struggle. When nature collapsed his will-power broke. It is hard for a resolute character to surrender; but Anthony, in his now thrice-purified soul, met the spectre of self and slew it forever. Henceforth he would make no plans: he would be in mind and heart what Saint Francis expected of every one of his followers — what he might very soon be in reality if his fever continued—a corpse, to be disposed of entirely by God's will, as manifested through those placed over him.

It was thus while lying prone on African soil, beneath the knife of the hardest of all executions — the slaying of personal ambition by an irrevocable act of one's own will, no matter how holy the ambition and how well-counseled the plan — that Saint Anthony was martyred, not indeed by giving his drained body into the hands of the Moors, but by giving his tortured soul into the hands of God. He had set out in the fall of 1220; early in 1221, in obedience to his superiors, he took leave again for Portugal.

He must have shrunk from this return. For being made humble does not mean that you have no sense of humiliation: it means rather that, despite a very keen repugnance, you carry to issue the task that steeps you in embarrassment. He would not have been human had his heart not sunk within him at the thought of meeting again in a few weeks those Canons Regular from whom he had so lately set out with an expedition of beggars in quest of souls for Christ and martyrdom for himself. As he stood by the ship's side and the tang from the salty waters of the Mediterranean swept over him, strength came back to his limbs and color crept into his cheeks. And his sensitive soul and vivid imagination must have pictured to him with maddening clarity the wise looks and head-noddings and I-told-you-so's awaiting him. For we have all found it hard to come back and lamely tell our story of failure: it has cost us a bloody sweat to walk down the home street on the day after our dismal return, to feel the eyes of smug wisdom pierce us from behind curtains and to force ourselves to accept pity from those by whom our folly was foretold.

This humiliation was spared Saint Anthony — and we heartily rejoice for him that it was. That same magnificent-looking Mediterranean, beneath the dazzling play of its surface, was on the verge of a tantrum. The storm broke, and poor Anthony's ship was driven from its course and washed up on the shore of Sicily. Amid the raging of waves and creaking of timbers, he stepped ashore in a strange land and made his way to the Franciscan House in Messina. He remained here about two months, gaining strength day by day as he walked in the garden or out along the seacoast in quiet meditation. It is said that he here planted a lemon tree that still flourishes.

Then news came down to this far-away end of Italy one morning to the effect that Saint Francis had called together another General Chapter of his Order in Assisi. Saint Anthony and a young lay Brother, also a saint, set out on their long, tedious journey northward.

5

Alone
Amidst Three Thousand

WHEN the five brethren whose martyred remains lay in state in the Monastery of Holy Cross at Coimbra, set out for Morocco, Francis of Assisi and twelve brethren set out for Egypt. At the Chapter of 1219 there had been an apportionment of Moslem territory: Brother Giles was to lead the spiritual attack on Tunis; Brother Vitale, on Morocco; Brother Francis was to march on to the spiritual conquest of Egypt, where a crusade was actually besieging Cairo at the moment. Franciscan history might have been written very differently had Brother Francis remained at home — but that belongs to another story.

Francis and his companions went on their march by way of Cyprus and Syria and on down to the delta of the Nile. And on this expedition the loyal, noble, generous, truth-loving soul of Francis was to receive a shock. Throughout his life he had yearned to be a crusader, to join in the heroic cause that was consuming Europe. His ambition was at last gratified and he was soon in the camp of the Christian army beneath the very walls of

Cairo.   Once there, however, it did not take Francis long to become disillusioned, to learn that a movement may start crystal-pure at its source, and yet, sadly, soon become defiled from the sordidness of man's ambitions that filter into it as it broadens and runs its way.   Every flow that goes to swell a stream does not add to the water's purity; and every new agency that gives fresh strength to a cause good in its beginning, does not necessarily contribute idealism in proportion to its influence.   In Egypt Francis learned, and learned quickly, Father Cuthbert tells us in his biography (*Life of Saint Francis of Assisi*), that the primitive crusading spirit had degenerated, so that, "for the most part, the Cross was a mere war cry, and the vision which beckoned the crusaders onward was a purely secular love of adventure, or worse still, lust of plunder and the vicious liberty of the camp."   Francis saw that Christ must be not only taught to the Mohammedan, but also retaught to the Christian crusaders who were struggling with the Mohammedan for Christ's sake.

He remained in the camp for some time, and then, after a heavy defeat sustained by the Christians, made his way one day through the army lines and into the tent of the Sultan, Malek-el-Khamil.   The gesture was typical; and the Sultan was won by Francis' personal charm.   In the course of the few meetings that they had, Malek came to feel a genuine admiration for this new type of crusader. He even pressed Francis to remain with him in his court. Francis refused the offer; and the attempt at converting the Mohammedan leader brought nothing better than a tender of beautiful gifts, and a free pass through Palestine. He refused the gifts; and when the crusaders a little later took Cairo, looted it, and, to avail ourselves again of Father Cuthbert's description, "succumbed to the seductive pleasures of the Egyptian spring, Francis . . . in sheer despair of doing any good there, turned his back on the crusade and, taking advantage of the spring sailings, crossed the sea to Acre." He visited the sacred places of Palestine and returned to Assisi, bringing with him Brothers Peter of Catania, Elias, Provincial of Syria, and Caesar of Speyer. Peter became his Vicar General on his return, but died soon after the appointment. Elias, as we see later, succeeded him. It was Caesar who helped Francis to rewrite his Rule, and who led the second expedition of Franciscans into Germany.

These years were filled with general disillusionment for the poor Saint of Assisi. He had seen the glory of a crusade wilt and drop in the enervating air and twisted back-streets of Cairo; he returned to Italy to find his brethren engaged in unedifying political squabbles, and the pristine, poetic, evangelical simplicity of his Rule becoming tarnished. He straightway went to Rome and obtained from Pope Honorius III a Cardinal Protector and Adviser for his Order. This was Ugolino, the Lord Cardinal of Ostia.

To bring the affairs of the Order back into harmony, Francis needed a helper, someone possessing a strong hand for discipline and a well-balanced mind for judgment. His choice fell on Elias — the worst choice, probably, ever made. Saint Francis selected for his Vicar General the man who came near to wrecking the whole Franciscan ideal.

Though Elias of Cortona belongs more to a life of Saint Francis than to this story of Saint Anthony, his influence on the whole Order was so colossal that a description of the man is almost necessary in the biography of an early Franciscan. Besides, there is the legend, take it for what it is worth, that at a later date, Saint Anthony actually upbraided Elias to his face.

Elias built the basilica that commemorates Saint Francis in Assisi, and Father Cuthbert has used the edifice to describe the man. "More or less rightly," he says, "the Sacro Convento has been taken to express the mind and life-purpose of the man who now became the administrator of the fraternity . . . . It is at once a great achievement and a failure. In itself it is so subtly woven of gracefulness and strength; laughing to scorn, as it does, the hindrances which the site first put in the way of its

construction and rising from the declivities in beauteous
freedom.   Truly a noble example of art: yet lacking the
supreme glory of art!   Did it but show in its superb
strength some feeling for the sublime unworldliness which
it professes to honor, it would have been a perfectly con-
gruous expression of the world's homage.   But the
building conveys no such feeling; it reveals no expression
toward what itself is not.   It is essentially self-contained,
demanding attention not for what it is not, but for what
it is.   It makes no confession of the greater glory of him
(Saint Francis) whose body it enshrines; rather it claims
his glory as an appendage of its own.   And so the Sacro
Convento — perfect in most things that make for per-
fection in art — bears a mark of insincerity and vanity;
and whilst its beauteous strength dominates your senses,
your soul is apt to be depressed: a sense of tragedy falls
upon you — at first you hardly know why.

"Much the same complexity of feeling and the same
final emotion comes to one in looking back upon Elias
himself.   There is a certain fascination in the broad
sweep of his ambition, in the strength of purpose which
made him, the son of an artisan, become the trusted coun-
selor and ambassador of Pope and Emperor and the
virtual ruler of the citizens of Cortona.   He went far
toward making the Franciscan Order a world-power,
throwing its influence into the world of politics and into

the intellectual life of the rising universities and into the mission-fields of Moslem territory."

Here we have the well-drawn picture of Elias, deep as to its shadows and sorrowfully articulate in its highlights. Elias almost made the Franciscan Order a world-power; but after all, is this to the credit of an institution whose chief influence was designed to be over emotions and aspirations directly concerned with the world to come? He more nearly took from the Franciscan Order all its power. He was a man of purely natural genius handling an ideal that sprang from the mystic heart of a purely supernatural genius. And as Saint Anthony came up from Africa and stood in the throng around the Portiuncula in the May of 1221, this is the man at whose feet sits the physically weakened figure of Saint Francis, at whose well-made habit the Seraphic Beggar tugs, into whose worldly ear the Poverello whispers the message he wishes delivered to the three thousand brethren gathered before him.

Saint Anthony could naturally know little of the ramifications of politics or of the various internal troubles that were beginning to disturb an Order about ten years old and having members throughout the world. The very nature of Francis' idealistic, primitive Rule of life made it inevitable, human nature being what it is, that difficulties of this character should beset the continuing expansion of the Order having that Rule for its charter and springing itself from the soul of the greatest troubadour and mystic this world has seen. Saint Francis was the poet of love and the beggar of Christ. Impatient of legal details, he and his first companions were content to gaze on and weep over the Crucified, satisfied to live by a Rule approved verbally by the pope. But quite necessarily the dragnet of vocations, real and imaginary, would bring into this life many men for whom the simple regulations founded and fostered by self-sacrifice would not suffice.

So we can easily understand that it was a somewhat mystified Anthony who stood in a strange land, a stranger amidst these men, and attended the meetings and councils that were shaping the future of a great institution. Among other minutes of the meetings he heard suggestions made for more crusades to foreign lands. This time he held his peace. God had brought to naught his first effort, and he was not going to tempt the issue a second time. When, at the close of the Chapter, Elias stood up and asked for volunteers for the German mission, Saint Anthony was not amongst the ninety "that arose and offered themselves to death." Caesar of Speyer, who was a German himself, and already known to his countrymen, took for the second attempt into this part of Europe twenty-five men out of the ninety who volunteered.

With this last detail attended to, the Chapter broke
up. Each man had been given his particular directions
and appointment; and three thousand Friars started for
their respective countries and duties. When the crowd
had melted away Saint Anthony stood alone, unknown,
unnoticed, without any appointment, companion, immediate superior or instructions. The young doctor of
the law, the recent Canon Regular, whose learning and
opinions were known and respected in the capital of his
native Portugal, stood apart, evidently not wanted by any
superior in this large brown assembly. He was dread-
fully alone amidst three thousand of his own brothers.

What a different history the Franciscan Order would
have had, had God inspired Saint Francis to come down
through the great throng of his spiritual sons, take the
hand of this young scholar and saint from Lisbon and
place him in the chair of authority on which he had just
seated Elias! How the slightest wish of the holy founder
would have been translated! How the primitive idealism
would have flourished under the guidance of this young
man whom men now call "the eldest son of Saint Francis"!

But dreams are only dreams, and often for our peace
of mind we should be better without them; for when
we wake, the realities are so much the duller from their
contrast with the rosy creatures our imagination created
and clothed for us. Our dreams are the land wherein

possibilities grow, the land in which we rule and reign, and wishes immediately become forces under our hand, while our lives are the realities wherein we are often the puppet in another's game. But we wish that someone at least had noticed Saint Anthony in the crowd.

It is an evidence of his recent resolution to leave his future in the hands of God, that he made no effort to receive an appointment in this Chapter. His heart and will belonged to Him in a contract made with his waning breath in Morocco. Besides, in a strange way he was already repaid for all his doubts, changes, labors and disappointments: for there in front of him stood Francis of Assisi. On the greensward of the Portiuncula, within a few grass-covered steps of each other, stood the two men that the world has taken to its mercurial heart. Anthony gazed on the emaciated face of him about whom he had heard so much in Coimbra, Africa and Messina; and as he gazed the centuries rolled backward and he was looking on Him of Whom Saint Francis is man's best copy. Kindness, gentleness, suffering, made the pale face of the Seraph winsome in its sadness; and despite the throng of strangers who moved around him deep in their own conversation, Saint Anthony was not alone in the real sense of the word; for we are never alone when we are in the presence of, in communion with, our ideal.

Anthony saw before him in the flesh him whose voice

had traveled across the hills and set him free: and during the days of the Chapter, whatever may have been his reactions to the squabbles the Friars were thrashing out among themselves, whatever doubt of his wisdom in joining this new Order may previously have come into his mind when the great ambition of his life failed, whatever questions may have troubled his soul regarding his ultimate lot amongst these men, the hours he had spent looking into the unforgettable face of Francis had dissolved. Besides, they were bringing him quickly to the climax of a newly growing desire.

As the last of the Franciscans were departing, Anthony bestirred himself and tugged at the sleeve of one who was passing. The Friar stopped and smiled: Anthony begged to be taken with him, whoever he was and whithersoever he might be going, and instructed in the mode of life this Francis had modeled for his followers so exactly on the life and virtues of Christ. The man Saint Anthony accosted happened to be Father Gratian, the gentle, lovable Provincial from Bologna. He heard Anthony's entreaty, embraced him in genuine gladness of spirit, and took him home to his own province in Romagna.

6

What the
Mountains Whispered

MOST men possessing what is commonly called the poetic soul have yearned for solitude, and even the rest of us who have just a soul have at times looked longingly toward the sea, the woodland islands, the blue depths of the mountains; have lifted our heads from amongst the machinery and listened for a second to the call of the trail; have taken our burning eyes from the loom and ledger for a period of time that men call a moment but which is really an aeon, and gazed hungrily up a tree-arched stream, across a loon-haunted lake, gazed in rapture at a vision that drifted into our lives we know not whence. There is no hunger like that hunger which we see yearly in the eyes of our country's tired millions as they start off each Saturday afternoon in summer for seashore and mountain trail. One lung-filling breath of freedom, one look on heaving sea or sleeping hill, one moment's stillness caught from the great silences of nature — these are what sustain men, and make a week's, a year's, hard, suffocating grind endurable.

Nature has a tonic for man's weary soul in her silences which are eternal, and for his jaded vision in her sleep which is illimitable.   When our artificial clinics fail to touch to fresh life a fretted mind and drooping body, day and night beneath the open sky, and wind on the heath and the tang of pines on the hill can whip back blood to a rounding cheek and fan to points of flame a fire that was dying in lacklustre eyes.

We acknowledge that this is a commonplace: but it has never seemed to us an illuminating practice in reading or talking to allude consistently to things of which most people are ignorant.   Mystifying utterances bring a hazy glory to the writer but no clarity or comfort to the reader.   Men, since the beginning, have gone to nature to build up broken bodies and remold shattered souls.   All men know the magic of the open sea when the wind runs up the green valleys of water and the white spume leaps high.   All men know the tonic of the mountains, and it is precisely because they do that they will fully appreciate the influence which the mountains had on the weary body and soul of Saint Anthony.

Some biographers have exercised their souls much in giving us reasons why he should have retired to a hermitage.   To us it seems wholly natural, considering all that went before it, and the change that had transformed the Canon Regular seeking martyrdom, and actually setting the tides of circumstance toward that ambition. In view of this and the fact that Saint Anthony was a new Franciscan at a General Chapter, depending for his appointment absolutely on the will of his highest superior, it is not strange that he should seek a place in which to reassemble his thoughts once more. It was providential that he went with Father Gratian.

It is quite a distance from Assisi to Bologna, especially when you go on foot: and nothing is more natural than that, on the way thither, Saint Anthony and his Provincial should have had many conversations. It is the duty of any superior to find out what talents and aspirations his subject possesses: and Father Gratian, in accepting this young man for his province, would naturally feel that he should discover, as far as possible, the actual merit of his disciple. Besides, Saint Anthony had belonged to another Order, had changed his manner of life, had come from Portugal, had been to Morocco, and had traveled up through the Italian Peninsula. Human curiosity, of which we are not told that Father Gratian was absolutely devoid, would prompt questions regarding Saint Anthony's hopes and mentality, and as the Provincial learned more and more about his desires, his admiration for him would grow: he would come to see that here was one soul hand-picked from amongst a million, one in whom the highest idealism of Saint Francis himself showed fruitful signs of being realized. To go ahead of our story a little for a moment, we might say that it was probably because he remembered many of the things about Saint Anthony which he had learned on this journey, that Father Gratian decided to call on him for the famous sermon at the ordination ceremony at Forlì— of which we shall speak later.

On the other hand, as we have noticed, Saint Anthony had undergone a transformation within the last year. The mysticism and beauty of his soul were developing, and he was at the point of greatest need for that meditation and quiet in which his heart would find more fully the Object of its love and lately stirred yearning, and his worn-out body regain its strength. Father Gratian had in his province the exact spot for such a man and for such a retreat. It was a hermitage on the very top of a range of mountains — Monte Paolo; and as soon as they arrived at his home, Father Gratian sent Anthony to this place.

It was here, we might say, that Saint Anthony became a Franciscan. Here he went through a novitiate in which he pondered and accepted the ideals whose following through the rest of his life led men to call him the eldest son of the Seraph of Assisi. He learned here and practised here the virtues peculiarly loved by Francis — humility, poverty, love of prayer and contemplation based entirely on the Crucified.   He was taught by no mortal teacher, but by Him Who, amidst the crags of La Verna and in the silence of the Portiuncula, had taught Saint Francis himself.

These mountains with their blue distances and deep caverns held the balm Saint Anthony's soul needed; and with their pure air, which his fever-parched body drank in, his mind too drank deep of the meditations so much in keeping with the place.   With bare head and naked feet he stood on the summit of this lordly range, steeped his soul in the infinite sweep of earth and sky, and loved God the more for His beauty and providence as here reflected.   And the mountains whispered to him their old, old teachings, as they had to Bernard and Francis and Benedict; as they had to the soul of their own Creator, of Him Who often "went into the mountains to pray." Saint Anthony has been called the Father of Mystic Theology; and who shall say by what deep scores in his mind and heart these lonely mountains instilled in him this second sight in the science of God?

However, mysticism without the accompanying practical virtues would very soon land the mystic in a mere poetic wonderland; the theology it inspired would be nothing better than fairy tales.   In the spiritual life, dreams without action are merely a sign of sleep.   None knew this better than Saint Anthony, who was taught by the Holy Spirit Himself. So we have Anthony at this time undergoing the most rigorous penances, seeking out and performing the most humiliating duties.

The hermitage on this mountain peak was poor indeed: yet it was not poor enough for the young Saint who was learning more thoroughly every day the poverty and sufferings of Christ. However, near the house was a grotto, or natural cave, in a high and wind-swept pine grove, and this bare classroom of heroic sanctity Saint Anthony made his ultimate retreat house. After his Mass and morning conferences each day he returned to this library of rocks and poverty to study deeper the love of God for man, to read a little further in the wondrous story of our redemption. A piece of dry bread and a little water sufficed for his daily fare. He remained on his knees for hours during the day, and knelt in meditation on through the night. And when the little bell that called the community to any exercise rang out in the thin air, Anthony would rise and totter — he was so weak at times he required a Brother's support — to whatever service or refection he was summoned.

Even this was not enough. He made a startling discovery one day: he was of no use in this hermitage. Its other members were cooking or questing or working, but he was doing nothing in payment for the food he was consuming! Genuine virtue is sharp-eyed toward self in these matters. As far as we can gather, the rest of the community were lay Brothers: Anthony was a priest, and therefore superior of the hermitage. But one day he appeared in the kitchen and asked the cook to let him help with the dishes and clean up the table and wash the floor after dinner.

Thus we have a descendant of the Bouillons on his knees in a scullery. We have a doctor of the law and the hereditary Governor of Lisbon reduced to the last stages of hunger and humiliation. To this plight he has come, led to the same objective physical privation as that to which the prodigal son in the Gospel was led. Saint Anthony arrived by the road of love, of poverty and suffering for Christ: the prodigal son came by the route of love of pleasure and pride in himself. But in the abyss of humiliation, saint and sinner meet: nor does the saint shun the sinner; nor is the sinner afraid to speak and confide his sorrow to a saint like this. As Christ, to save the sinner, stripped Himself and humbled Himself to the position wherein He took on His shoulders the burden of atonement and the cross of a malefactor, thus making it easy for sinners to approach Him, so the saints have ever thrown away all pomp and mental pride and have come down to the ordinary man's level, making humble confession easy for all who have, through human weakness, erred and wandered far.

This retreat in the mountains was the eclipse before the dawn. Soon from this craggy peak a light would break that would bathe the plains of Italy and the fields of France in a noonday of splendor, and travel down through the ages in a great, white, illuminating ray. Soon from this cave in the pine-clad fastnesses of Romagna would emerge a lion mighty in his strength, the confidence of victory in his royal pose. Taught by the mountains in their strong, eternal silences, nurtured by them in their rock-ribbed surety, Saint Anthony the preacher came forth on his mission, his voice carrying the deep resonance of the canyon-born cry, and his heart the living peace and divine sympathy that he himself had received, and that had made him whole.

7

When Others Decline

WHEN everybody unanimously refuses a public task, it is, as a rule, because it involves something alarming to self-love — criticism, perhaps, or acute embarrassment. The man who offers himself for exhibition under these circumstances possesses a peculiarly fine grade of humility. And just as there is something weak, cowardly and contemptible in the huddled fear of mob ridicule, so there is something captivating and heroic in an upright and outstanding effort to do one's best and be laughed at for the attempt. We love such people, I suppose, because we secretly admire him who has the courage to try what we were too timid to try.

Whatever the psychology of the matter may be, the facts have not changed through the centuries. It fell out one day in the affairs of the Friars Minor that there was an ordination at Forlì, not far from Monte Paolo. Franciscans and Dominicans from neighboring villages and hermitages were invited. Quite an assembly of clerics gathered in the sanctuary to witness the sacred and touching ceremonies in which young men were being raised to the dignity of the priesthood. It was as imposing then as now: the bishop in his falling lace and sweeping train, the prelates in their distinguished colors, the monks and Friars in their characteristic browns and blacks and whites.

At collation, the Franciscan superior cast around him for a man to give the customary address. His eye rested on the Brother Preachers. But as he went from one to another, with the request that each deliver the sermon, each looked at the bishop sitting at the top table, at the rows of faces around — and then declined the honor. The superior next appealed to certain others present; but each gave a cogent and admirably logical explanation of why he in particular was not the proper speaker for such an occasion. Father Gratian turned lastly to his own men, as was fitting in the matter of bestowing honors; only to make the discovery that the Brothers, too, were not in a discoursive mood that day. Not one in the whole assembly could see any reason why he, of all people, should have to preach. Father Gratian was beginning ruefully to think that if there was to be a sermon at all, he himself would have to give it, when his eye fell on Brother Anthony. Here was a man who had courted martyrdom; it was just possible that he might be induced to come to the rescue.

Approaching the young hermit, he whispered his plight. Anthony at first refused with the story of unworthiness that sounded very much like the others he had heard. But Father Gratian was inspired this time, and presently Anthony stood up.

When the shifting and stir had subsided, he had received the bishop's blessing and was in the pulpit, for better or for worse. He took for his text the very words of Holy Scripture that must have prompted him to accept this duty as a matter of obedience to his superior: "Christ became obedient unto death, even unto the death of the Cross."

At first his voice was low and tremulous, we are told; nor are we surprised, for it takes even a saint a few minutes to compose himself when confronted with such an interested and learned audience. As the moments passed, however, Anthony found his voice, struck his stride, launched into his theme: he had lost forever that which has choked many a young speaker — and he delivered the most stirring first-Mass sermon these assembled priests and prelates had ever heard.

The theme was the priesthood: and as Anthony spoke of Christ and His royal Priesthood, his pale, thin face shone with an interior light. He laid heavy tax on the Scriptures, and poured forth the inspired utterances of the prophets. He aligned the Fathers; and each, as he

was called in, gave testimony of the sanctity and dignity
conferred by the great High Priest on the office which
these young men before him had received. Anthony's
artistic imagination, piercing intellect and colossal memory wove from the diversely gathered material a word-
tapestry of the enduring priestly life of Christ.

All were amazed, of course; and emotion was warm
in the handclasps of congratulation. But if there was
one man beside himself with delight, that man was
Father Gratian. What a precious stone he had picked
up in the hills of Umbria and brought back to the hills
of Lombardy! How he was vindicated for taking in this
stranger! No more time should be lost in giving Anthony
his proper introduction to the world. Not another minute should be spent till this incomparable gem was in its
right setting. It was cut with a facet to catch every
human appeal, cut to reflect the red fire of love that was
burning so brightly in its center. And Father Gratian
would see to it that the world should behold this
sparkling treasure.

He immediately conferred on the young hermit the
faculty of preaching to the people. And it was thus
that Anthony stepped forth from his cell of rocks into
the pulpits of Lombardy and France and Padua.

It is useless to speculate; but speculation, like every
other useless pastime, makes a winning appeal to most

of us.   What would have happened had Anthony refused
the pleadings of his superior to preach at the ordination
in the town of Forlì?   Sooner or later he would have
been discovered, probably.   But we should have lost one
of the most chivalrous touches in the history of his life.
For while we admire him for the beauty of his sermon,
our heart goes out to him in genuine love for stepping
into the breach and saving a man from embarrassment.
We warm to the tender human loyalty that stood by a
friend in need.

It is true that no great issue was involved in the
preaching of one sermon more or less.   But it is because
the issue was not great that we admire him for making
it happy.   Probably if it had been a matter of great concern, like a fire or a sudden death, any priest in the
assembly would have come to the help of Father Gratian.
But it is in the little things of life that we notice real
friends; even strangers will assist in noticeable distress.
It is in our trifling annoyances and petty losses that Saint
Anthony has often been tender enough to help us.   A
mislaid key, a lost book, a forgotten street number—these
are not national calamities; but they fret us and can spoil
our happiest day.   It is precisely in these that Saint
Anthony carries on that generous, thoughtful, understanding help he tendered the superior in the convent of Forlì.
It is only the very greatest of souls that can thus see our

detailed wants and embarrassments.   "Give us this day
our *daily* bread," begged Christ for us.   "They have no
wine," whispered the mother of Jesus when her eye,
quick for the minute needs of others, noticed that a young
couple were about to be humiliated before their guests
at their wedding supper.

8

Brother Anthony, My Bishop

SOME men have uttered a kind of sincere non-sense about Saint Francis' views on learning that has fairly successfully clouded the point. On the other hand, some have written so lucidly on the matter that not to quote them verbatim is to resist a very strong temptation. To carry on with our story we must here devote a few words to this subject, which belongs rather to Saint Francis' life: a few, not because our casual glance has penetrated the cloud that has baffled so many earnest scholars, but following our original intention not to dwell on arguments that have a charm for scholars only. The phase of Saint Anthony's life we are now entering rests on this discussion, and we feel that we must give at least a summary of the case as we apprehend it.

Saint Francis was born in the very seed-time of the Renaissance. The conceits of learning had just begun to cast their alluring spell over a world awakening from intellectual unconsciousness. Most of us can recall a like period in our own personal lives. We can remember

those days, were we freshmen or were we seniors, culmi-
nating in that day of wisdom itself on which we held the
coveted parchment in our hands at last — when the possession of even the appearance of scholarship thrilled us
and made us vain. The grain was yet milk-soft in its
downy husk, and we thought it was hanging hard and
yellow on the stalk. The ensuing years have changed
all that, and have brought their disillusioning wisdom;
but they have not changed the fact that that time existed.

This, as nearly as a figure can describe it, was the
state of the intellectual world in Saint Francis' day. Men
set themselves to gain an education, yet too often their
aim and goal was only the "trappings and the suits" of
knowledge. The pretentiousness, the childish and self-
defeating vanity, of this attitude, was particularly abhorrent to the simple, mystical, sincere soul of Francis. He
saw the dangers that lay in these conceits, and he marked
them with peculiar insight when those pursuing them
were his brethren. He had no quarrel with learning, but
we must distinguish: he had no reverence for learning
followed for mere learning's sake; he praised learning
for God's sake. That was why he revered with peculiar
homage "all theologians", that is, men versed in the
science of God. It was the effect of newly-discovered,
unorientated and not very profound learning that he
feared on the simple piety of his brethren.

Superficially, the brethren had their case. So much power lay in education; it brought a sense of independence; it opened vast possibilities in politics; it was the highroad to positions in Church and State — at least so they thought. But Saint Francis was steadfast. He knew whither an education pursued for these reasons would lead. He had not learned this by progressive analysis; he sensed it, felt it intuitively. He set his own sincere face against it; and time and again he pulled the mask from the face of pseudo-education.

Of course Saint Francis actually grasped the need of learning infinitely more clearly than the others; while they were content with what a consciousness awakening from an age of lead was willing to call learning, he urged his followers on to that depth of knowledge wherein education finds itself humble again and ready to reach out and take the hand of God as its only sure guide. This is the type of learning he has in mind when he cautions his brethren not to let study destroy their spirit of prayer. He knew that study should be the highest form of prayer, especially study of the sacred sciences; and he knew that the awakening love of learning was not working out precisely in that way.

There was a case in point. While Francis was in the East his Provincial, Peter Stacia, had built a school at Bologna, then a seat of learning; and in this school the raw reverence to the mere appearance of education was being devoutly offered by certain of the Franciscan brethren. Moreover, the spirit that Francis most feared had worked out here exactly as he had dreaded; for the brethren of this house claimed the building as *their own property* — that very breach of poverty that Francis had always warned them would follow their cessation from humble prayer, would take possession of them as they raised the traitorous standard of worldly wisdom.

Saint Francis had hurried to Bologna when he heard of this state of affairs. Refusing to stay at the Franciscan house, he lodged with the Dominicans. He closed the college, took away all the Friars living therein, deposed and cursed the Provincial. This procedure not only caused comment; it was the beginning of Saint Francis' agony of mind. He realized that his priests must be taught — but where was he to find the teacher? What man was capable of the task? And now it was that ripples from the pebble dropped in the pool at Forlì broke around the chair of Elias and the kneeling-bench of Francis.

There was in the very province of the Romagna, he had heard of late, a young Franciscan who, through a sermon delivered at Forlì during an ordination, and subsequent preaching in several local missions, had been discovered to possess the very type of mind that Saint

Francis yearned to see in his teacher. He was, it appeared, a man whose deep mystic knowledge of God did not ignore speculative knowledge, but rather united with it in a glowing lucidity of thought and expression; a man in whom there was a yearning "for the vision of truth rather than for its analysis"; who by moral and intellectual training and by the cast of his personality united intuition and logic, dogma and poetry, head and heart. It was Anthony of Lisbon. He was later called by Pope Gregory IX the father of mystic theology. And we may say, by way of parenthesis, that Saint Bonaventure, some fifty years later, was the very out-flowering of this seed in the Franciscan system of theology.

Francis acted without delay. "Brother Anthony," he wrote, "my Bishop, it pleases me that you should read sacred Theology to the brethren so long as on account of this study they do not extinguish the spirit of holy prayer, as is ordained in the Rule. Farewell."

Though our treatment of Saint Francis' attitude toward learning has been necessarily short, we hope we have made clear the implications of the confidence he reposed in Anthony by thus appointing him the first teacher of the Order. Let us remember, in sad contrast, that he had cursed another who had attempted to found a school and to work himself into the position of its master in Bologna.

Armed with his commission, Anthony set out for the university city; not to take the chair of the theological faculty there, for no such thing existed yet; but simply to impart to his own brethren the knowledge necessary for the priesthood.

Slight though this appointment seems to us now, it marked a great evolution in the Franciscan mode of life; for the Friar Preachers of the future were to be no mere untrained men speaking of the love of Christ Crucified from hearts bursting with that love. They were to add the scientific knowledge of theology to their personal qualities and native holiness. We may regret the passing of the old simplicity, but we must recognize that it was inevitable. Anthony and the band of preachers he led were to speak not only to the peasant folk of Umbria, to simple, common, untutored hearts of the hills, but to men who were laughing outright at ecclesiastical authority and sneering openly at holiness.

It was entirely fitting, therefore, that the preachers should be trained accurately for their work; and no man, of that age or any other, was better qualified to give this training than he who had probed deep in booklore under the instruction of the Canons at Holy Cross, and sounded the depths of seraphic love in the grotto of Monte Paolo under the inspiration of Francis of Assisi. Anthony possessed a native intellectual bent and a brilliantly informed mind, the fruits of which he would inevitably impart to his pupils. He realized, moreover, that the time was ripe for arguments based on a speculative knowledge of God, the universe, the facts of life, and the appetites and needs of body and soul. But he also knew, both from inner wisdom and practical personal experience, that personal holiness was, everywhere and always, the best eloquence.

One case may be cited to illustrate this. There lived at Rimini on the sea a man possessed of a mule and a heresy; the latter was of some thirty years' standing, the former was hungry and in the prime of life. The man's name was Bononillo; his dogmatic unbelief was centered on the Blessed Sacrament. Anthony went to Rimini on one of his missions. He and Bononillo met. He recounted to the heretic the arguments demonstrating Christ's Real Presence under the appearance of bread, as they are found in Scripture and in the writings of the Fathers. Yet Bononillo was not convinced. Anthony looked at him and at the mule which he was leading. Then he made an offer. Let Bononillo keep the animal fasting for three days and then bring it to the public square. Anthony would be there on one side, holding the Blessed Sacrament; on the other side would be set a tempting feed. If the mule refused to eat, and, instead, bowed down before the Blessed Sacrament, would Bononillo believe? Bononillo would. Anthony merely made the stipulation that, if the miracle should not come to pass, his sins alone were to be blamed. At the designated time the heretic appeared with the mule; and the animal, despite its consuming hunger, turned away from the food and, as if endowed with reason, bent its knees and remained with bowed head before the Sacred Host. Not to be outdone by his own mule, the heretic too knelt down, adored Christ under the appearance of bread, and gave up his heresy.

This was the type of man, then, that Anthony had to train his disciples to convert. First must be taught the whole store of scientific theology as possessed by that time; then must be added that spirit of prayer which Saint Francis continually urged. In learning were to be found the arguments based on reason, which men respect and demand since God has created the reasoning faculty in them, and which Christ continually used in His own preaching. In prayer was nurtured that faith which illuminates and convinces when mere human reason proves too weak.

These are the facts, the cold picture of Anthony the Teacher in the abstract. But we know that his eye, bright with a faith as clear and burning as our central sun, his face suffused with the light that spread glowing from a life of purity and penance, his tongue eloquent with the fire that seven hundred years have not extinguished — we know that these were what helped most to lead his pupils along the path of holiness and learning. These were what first exemplified to the world that vital ideal entwined with the crossed arms of Christ and Francis in the motto of Franciscan teachers: *In sanctitate et doctrina.*

9

Anthony
Among the People

A NTHONY had a message for the Bononillos; and if they were not willing to give ear, then he would preach it anyhow — to the flowers, or to the fishes, or to the mules, or to any other part of creation he happened to think of. And it chanced that there were a great many Bononillos in Lombardy at that time, and that their gathering place was Rimini.

But now we must drive in a few isolated historical pegs before we can begin to cover securely with the tent of our story this period of Anthony's life.

Peg the first: A Persian named Zoroaster, who lived about 600 B. C., reduced the existing hallucinations that passed for philosophy in the India and Persia of his day to two heads, or two principles — the good and the evil. The good force would conquer the evil, he calculated, after a struggle of twelve thousand years; because the evil force was working blindly, and in the dark. The good force presided over day and light and sunshine and the positive things of life; the evil force held reign over night, death, matter in general and all negations. The

name of the good god or principle was Ahura-Mazda:
his name is perpetuated for us in electric bulbs. People
now know the great Mazda as the scullion of man. The
evil principle was called Angra-Mainyu — and nobody
now amongst us but the learned knows that he ever
existed under such a fine name. This is the beginning
of the famous dual principles, two supreme beings
always at war. The theory has havoc to work yet.

Peg the second: In the third century after Christ
there lived a Persian convert called Manes who saw fit
to introduce into Christian theology and philosophy
Zoroaster's conception of the dualism of God and matter.
Manes was helped somewhat by a sect known as the
Gnostics, who held that Christ taught His apostles certain inside doctrines that He hid from the common
people. The doctrine of Manes is called, after him,
Manichaeism. It is simply, to repeat, the projection into
Catholic thought of the notion of two forces at work
for supremacy.

"There is no doubt that Manes' followers, in developing the teachings of the founder of the sect, were
influenced to a large extent by the Gnostic dualism, and
laid claim, as the Gnostics did, to a special *gnosis*.
They concerned themselves chiefly with *the problem of
evil,* assuming the existence of two eternal principles,
the one essentially good and the other essentially evil,

and deriving from the latter all the evil, physical and moral, which exists in the world.   They maintained that from the good principle there emanated in the first place, primeval man, who was the first to enter into the struggle with evil; in the next place, the Spirit of Life, who rescued primeval man from the powers of darkness: finally the World-Soul, Christ, the Son of primeval man, who restored to man the light which he had lost in the struggle with darkness.   They distinguished in man two souls — the soul that animates the body, and the soul of light, which is part of the World-Soul, Christ.   The former is the creation of the powers of darkness, the latter is an emanation from the light itself.   Thus, man's soul is a battlefield on which light and darkness are at war, as they are in the universe.   Human action depends on the outcome of the contest: there is no freedom of choice. All matter is evil and the cause of evil" (*A History of Philosophy,* by William Turner, S. T. D.).   Saint Augustine, before his conversion, was a Manichaean.   He later refuted their so-called philosophy.

Peg the third: About the eleventh century, two factions of Manichees, the Paulicians and the Bogomils, came from the East, set themselves up in northern Italy and called themselves Cathari — a Greek word meaning Puritan.   Their practical belief and observance was this: "They believed in the migration of souls, and accordingly refused to put any animal to death; they refrained from worshiping in churches, rejected the sacraments, the veneration of pictures and crosses; they also considered oaths, wars, the death punishment and civil government to be unlawful. They likewise abstained from marriage and from flesh-meat (though not from fish), and even from eggs and milk (though not from wine), and observed long and severe fasts" (*A Manual of Church History,* by Dr. F. X. Funk).

Later they spread into France. This branch (now known as the Albigenses, from the town of Albi, in southern France), held to absolute dualism: two gods, two worlds, two principles — good and evil. Those who remained in northern Italy held generally to the teaching that evil came not from a god but from a fallen spirit called Satan; that is, they held Satan to be a *principle* of evil.

A sect known as the Waldenses added to the general confusion in Lombardy. These, too, held distorted notions of poverty and the evangelical virtues, and recruited most of their followers from the impoverished ignorant. This was natural, for these poor people were least fitted to detect their evils and errors. Add, finally, the Arnoldists, who had a special grudge against priests and bishops — and the pegs are almost ready for the ropes and canvas.

We need just one more, the fourth: Two towns in Germany gave their respective names to two factions that contributed political and military bewilderment and corruption to the north of Italy: the towns of Welf and Waiblingen. When the bearers of these names crossed the Alps, of course no Italian could pronounce them, so the Lombards called them Guelphs and Ghibellines. The trouble between these two places had started originally when Henry the Proud, of the House of Welf, expected the Empire of Lothair, which Conrad III of the House of Hohenstaufen actually received. Henry's brother, Count Welf, was besieged in Weinburg. The defenders had "Welf!" for their battle-cry. The besiegers hailed from Waiblingen where Frederick, Duke of Swabia, Conrad's brother, was born; and as they charged they shouted, "Waiblins!" to strike terror into the besieged.

Waiblins, Waiblingen, Ghibelline, call it as you wish, this faction was the support of the Emperor. Welf, Guelph, it is all the same, this one upheld the Pope. The struggle between Pope and Emperor had its beginning when Frederick I — Barbarossa or Redbeard — had endeavored to retain imperial sway over Lombardy. The larger cities of Lombardy wanted freedom, and fought for it: they looked to the Pope for help, and got it. The Pope turned to the natural enemies of the Emperor—the Guelphs—to aid him. The Emperor appealed to his own backers. So into Lombardy trooped Guelphs and Ghibellines, took up the Italian cudgels and went merrily at each other's throats throughout Milan and Padua and the cities of northern Italy. That was about the middle of the twelfth century.

The politico-religious struggle continued unabated through the years. There were urgent reasons why each side felt it should conquer. The kingdom of Sicily then took in the whole lower half of the Italian Peninsula. Lombardy was the north. They were beginning to fall apart. Still, the Hohenstaufens were in Sicily; the Hohenstaufens were in Lombardy; and the Pope protested against the Patrimony of Peter being the meat in a Hohenstaufen sandwich.

It was the natural policy of the popes, first, to try their best "to keep the Sicilian Crown from being too closely united to the Empire", and, secondly, to keep the Emperor from controlling Lombardy. It was a game of chess, in which the papal territory might be "taken". The cities of northern Italy were the pawns; the Guelphs and Ghibellines were the bishops, kings, knights and rooks; the Pope and the Emperor were the players.

We remarked in a previous chapter that when Ferdinand Martini, a student at Holy Cross in Coimbra, heard of the crowning of Frederick II at Aix-la-Chapelle in 1215, he had hoped, with others, that it would advance the

Fifth Crusade and the settlement of the strife between the Papacy and the Empire. If Ferdinand the Augustinian had those hopes, Anthony the Franciscan would now be disappointed at the actual behavior of Frederick. He did not live, of course, to see Frederick the Excommunicate crown himself with his own hands King of Jerusalem, nor Frederick's subsequent hostility to the popes. Anthony would have been a canonized saint for eighteen years when Frederick II, in 1250, would meet his death in the age-old conflict of the century-old feud, raging at its height that year through the Romagna, with Guelph and Ghibelline still shouting their guttural battle-cries. Years afterward, the last of the Hohenstaufens would be executed at Naples; and the French supremacy of the Angevins, whom the popes sent to Sicily, would terminate in the tragic Sicilian Vespers.

Such are the figures that flitted through that dark and bloody period. It was with heretic, hypocrite, soldier and politician working, fighting and worming, each his devious way, to some fancied position of power or purse, that Saint Anthony had to deal. The tent can now be raised, and Anthony can ascend the pulpit and preach to the people.

And what a motley crowd are these that look up at him! Brigands, soldiers of fortune, strangers from beyond the Alps, heretics, men who believed in the confederacy, men ready to die for the union — such were his hearers. Barefooted fanatics, bare-headed dervishes, men who went back to Zoroaster for their beliefs, who taught all that was bad in Manichaeism, and called themselves Puritans, opposed him. Preachers with Milan for their Rome and Piedmont for their recruiting grounds, appeared, wearing the mask of the very virtues that Anthony was preaching, practising and exhorting all to follow. Apostates to faith and fatherland, who wanted a stranger to govern them and a Persian doctrine to give them license, sneered at him as he passed.

The society that Anthony had to reconstruct was shot through with the worst type of error, and reduced to anarchy and starvation by continuous war. The common people were very common indeed, yet they were his only hope. He and the band which he had instructed in that spirit of prayer demanded by Saint Francis, and in those arguments demanded by the state of things — he and this band of preachers had to go out into a mission field that was not so much white for the harvest as soiled for the washing. They had to start with fundamental things: had to teach that there is one only God, Creator of heaven and earth, all-powerful, all-wise, all-holy — and this to a people who were being taught that there were two gods; had to preach the sanctity and divinity of the Catholic Church to men who were being paid by the

Emperor to fight the Pope; had to preach the indissolubility of marriage to those who had learned from the Puritans of that day that all marriage is evil; had to inculcate respect for government in those who held that all civil government is unlawful; had to teach free will and personal responsibility to a just God to those who had been told the night before, between battles, perhaps, or during a gorged lull after looting a city, that man's soul is merely a neutral battlefield between two powers, and that individual actions depend on the outcome of that contest, with no freedom of choice left to the man.

"Following a perverted asceticism they [the Cathari or Puritans] condemned Christian marriage and taught that concubinage was preferable to marriage, because less permanent. In the minds of the untutored this teaching was taken to be a license for impurity. The astute saw in it a way of sinning in the very name of religion. The outcome was that the heresy was practically a campaign of vice. By name pure, in life vicious, lawless in fact, seditious in teaching — for which reason they endangered and antagonized the civil powers as well as the religious — they were working untold harm among the people" (*Saint Anthony in Life,* by Victor Sheppard, O. F. M.).

Saint Anthony, as has been seen, had had a striking encounter with one of them at Rimini; his biographers relate another incident at the same place. In preaching one day to this more than strange people, Anthony happened to hurt their feelings — no doubt either by his analysis of their vicious philosophy or by his denunciation of their perverted practices. At any rate, charged with fury at some part of his sermon, they rose *en masse,* and left the place with a loud clamor: just as the Jews had left Christ on several occasions when He hit at their pet corruptions and errors. Anthony found himself suddenly talking to space. An ordinary preacher, and even many extraordinary ones, would have shaken from their shoes the dust of such a place. But Anthony did not make converts that way. An idea struck him. Leaving the pulpit, he made his way to the river close by, and began to preach again — this time to the fishes. These creatures proved to be better Christians than the Cathari, for they listened, at least with outward reverence, to the Word of God. Others hurried from up-stream and downstream, gathered in a great shoal, cocked their heads sidewise above water, and remained in this devout posture till Anthony finished, blessed them and bade them go.

We do not know if any converts were made by this miracle: but if not, surely another miracle was wrought, of dulness, perversity and stupidity in the presence of such a manifestation of the divine commission shining forth in a man "preaching as one having power."

Thus the teacher whom Francis selected to be the first in his Order had not lost the spirit of simple, trusting prayer to which all other things must be subservient. He had something to say for man's benefit, something coming straight from God. He delivered his message as his followers delivered theirs through the centuries, to packed cathedrals in Europe, to solitary Indians in Peru. For Anthony had the heart of Francis of Assisi, and this he awakened in his Friar companions in turn — the heart that breathes that peculiar eloquence so simple in seeming, yet so hard to master. United with his marvelous learning, he had that power of direct utterance that reaches in clear rays through the dim intelligence of the simple folk and the unlettered. He had that unaffected clarity of speech which is always understood and appreciated by the common people whom he loved so much.

10

Anthony
Among the Preachers

"THE DISTANCE between these two men [Saint Francis and Saint Anthony] is as great as that which separates Jesus from Saint Paul" (Paul Sabatier). "Would the disciples of Saint Francis have had the same saving influence as their master if they had retained his methods of preaching? We do not think so. The Poverello owed his apostolic success to his saintliness, and perhaps also, to some extent, to the novelty of his preaching. But the people would soon have tired of this simple extempore method if the Minorite Friars had continued to employ it when preaching to them. Moreover, an uneducated preacher is usually a very poor one" (Albert Lepitre).

Whether we quarrel or agree with the statements just quoted — and Sabatier's, in the sense in which he meant it, is ridiculous — they show us clearly that an evolution in Franciscan preaching came with Saint Anthony and his followers; for both Sabatier and Lepitre are accurate reporters on Franciscanism. While we need not admit Sabatier's deductions, we must all admire his research into Franciscana; and Lepitre's is the best life of Saint Anthony we have seen to date.

Anthony preached for about two years in his own province of the Romagna, which then took in the whole of Lombardy. We have seen the type of character to which he had to appeal; and we have noted how a change in approach was demanded by the change of time and place. We shall see later how Saint Francis himself comprehended these things, and sent Anthony to southern France to uproot the heresy there, born twin to that growing up in lusty paganism in Lombardy.

If it is interesting to stand on a height of land and watch a crystal rill gurgle out from beneath a fungus-spotted rock, it is equally interesting to follow in fancy that rill to the sea. North or south it may run; it will grow as it goes, and here and there it may be polluted; it will give life to thirsty beasts and plants; it will serve man through the thousand tortures wherein he twists and chokes it to his own ends; it will carry ships of freight and ships of pleasure, and take children in its arms; it will finally meet the tide, and even then for many a mile between banks of green ocean water the rill, the river, will retain its individuality. So, for a short chapter, we shall glance at Anthony's preaching and its marvelous influence on Franciscan preachers — an influence that lasts to the present day.

Saint Francis preached a telling sermon. So did the Curé of Ars. But it would be suicidal for an ordinary man to copy either of these literally. Their personalities, that is, their personal genius and sanctity, spoke; their plain sincerity captivated all. A man would simply have to *be* Saint Francis, *be* the Curé of Ars, to preach like them. In other words, such men could never found a school or method of preaching. Their most telling force could not be taught nor transmitted to everyday pupils. Their style was native to the preachers, to the soil on which they stood. Would Saint Francis' method have been successful, even in Umbria, if any but him had attempted it? We must leave the question open, but we hardly think it would have been.

Which was why Anthony the student, living among heretics and impostors, was forced by internal qualities and external circumstances alike to give a new method and a new impetus to Franciscan preaching. He differs from Saint Francis not at all in essence; he merely casts his discourse in oratorical form. His is still the voice from Assisi, we might say; but a voice trained to run up and down the scale of rhetoric. It is still the crystal stream from the Umbrian hills, but it has received many tributaries from the right and from the left. And these additions are faculties, qualities, that other men can acquire. Anthony — and he was probably the only man in the Franciscan family capable of doing it — took Saint Francis' method of preaching and developed it without fundamentally changing it; engrafted on it all that the forensic art of his day had to offer, without uprooting or injury.

His description of the private life of a good missionary might, in fact, have been dictated by Saint Francis himself: "It behoveth a preacher to lead on earth a heavenly life in keeping with the truths he is charged to announce to the people. His conversation should only be concerning holy things, and his endeavors must tend to but one end: the salvation of souls. It is his duty to raise up the fallen, to console them that weep, to distribute the treasures of Divine grace as the clouds send down their refreshing showers. And all this must he do with perfect humility and absolute disinterestedness. Prayer must be his chief delight and the remembrance of the bitter Passion of the Son of God must ever accompany him whether in joy or adversity. If he acts .in this wise, the Word of God, the word of peace and life, of grace and truth, will descend upon and flood him with its dazzling light."

Innocence of life . . . humility . . . zeal for souls . . . a sympathy as broad as human misery and human joys . . . the Passion of Christ . . . peace . . . tranquillity . . . love of truth — they are of Francis; argument, appeal, figure, organization, balance, all used to communicate and develop the sense of those others — they are of Anthony. That is why Sabatier is wrong in saying that there is a separation between Saint Francis and Saint Anthony. There is not separation, but a marvelous continuity. To use our figure, Anthony's preaching is not another stream running parallel to that of Francis; it is the same stream, dug wide enough and deep enough by science and native talent to carry onward to the ocean of God's grace the freights and pleasure boats of man's making — boats that must be carried somehow, but never will be carried on an upland rivulet, no matter how crystal. A stream could never flow if it did not rise; it could never carry commerce if it did not grow. Francis is the rise, and Anthony the growth, of Franciscan homiletics.

"He had, to a remarkable degree, all those qualities which make a preacher: a loud, clear voice, a winning countenance, prodigious memory, profound learning, together with the spirit of prophecy and an extraordinary gift of miracles. Besides all these qualities, he was a saint. He undertook to reform the morals of an age in which luxury, avarice and tyranny were very prevalent. By his preaching, his zeal and fearless championing of the truth, he eradicated the heresies of the Cathari and Patarines, and for his extraordinary work against heretics he was called *Malleus Haereticorum* (The Hammer of

Heretics). No preacher of the Franciscans, or of any other order or congregation, was greater than Saint Anthony of Padua. Few approach him. This is a broad statement, but it is borne out by the facts. His audience numbered, at times, as many as thirty thousand people. Often after he had finished preaching, the number of penitents was so great that there were not enough priests in the vicinity to hear confessions. He preached vices and virtues, punishment and glory, with abundant fruits. It is almost superfluous to say that he was a successful preacher of the Word" (Boniface McConville, O. F. M., in *St. Bonaventure's Seminary Year Book,* 1927).

I will take the liberty of quoting here, at some length, from an article by Henry Kirk, published in the *Commonweal* for March 25, 1931. It has a fire all its own, which touches to brighter radiance the name of Anthony the preacher. "To very few," says Mr. Kirk, "is Anthony of Padua known as a biblical authority.... His true genius, which caused his canonization, was that of evangelical preaching. In this he has probably never been excelled in the Catholic Church."

He continues: "It is particularly interesting to comment upon Anthony's Lenten sermons at Milan, where the memory of the noted Bishop Ambrose had survived through eight succeeding centuries. This celebrated Bishop, who feared neither emperor nor Athens, was a

man of genuine distinction embastioned by Greek culture
as well as by Latin intellect. His *Apologia of the
Prophet David* could not have been unknown to
Anthony. At all events, the work had a revival with
Anthony's coming to Milan. There were new printings
and renewed discussion. Milan aroused by a Franciscan
Friar in the pulpit of the great Ambrose revived the days
of Ambrose, and to what effect! The great Bishop, his
honesty, his courage, his gentle homilies, his devotion to
the Gospel; the saintly Ambrose who made the flaming
Augustine await his final conversion; Bishop and administrator, seigneur and statesman, unconquerable prelate
— Ambrose, the glory of Milan, was outpreached by a
Franciscan Friar in a brown robe! It was not because
Anthony was more profound than Ambrose, nor a greater
theologian — both of which he happened to be. Nor
was it because of his youth, his vitality, his glittering pre-
sentment. Rather it was that he was an evangel — another, though very different, John the Baptist. What
the literati of Milan were saying one to another was
this: 'Here is an intellectual modern saint!' What the
unlaureled exclaimed one to another was this: 'Here
is a man of God!' What they all found, each in common with the other, was the Gospel given to them as
probably it never had been given before."
    So did it continue with Anthony of Padua through

all his days.   His appearance everywhere was an event.
Law courts and shops were closed that everyone might
have a chance to hear him.   Invariably, he was compelled
to address crowds in public squares, the cathedrals and
churches being wholly inadequate to hold the throngs of
his listeners.

And if Anthony introduced a method of preaching
into the Order, there were not wanting in the following
generations men to carry on the work.   Saint Peter of
Alcántara is probably the greatest penitential preacher
of history.   His personal fasts and austerities stagger
the mind;   Saint Teresa saw his soul go straight to
heaven when he died.   He was essentially a missionary
preacher, and he inaugurated the custom of erecting a
large crucifix in church during missions.   Berthold of
Ratisbon preached throughout Germany, Switzerland,
Austria and Bohemia.   Roger Bacon says this of him:
"Friar Berthold, in his missionary career, accomplished
more than all the preachers of the two great mendicant
Orders combined."   Roger Bacon was a man of choler,
but we can let a lot of blood from the statement and still
have a robust description left.   No church was large
enough to hold the congregation when Berthold preached.
He was a man of white sanctity in his personal life; and
his greatest homiletic faculty was his power of translating
abstruse thoughts into the language of the common

people. His sermon, *The Valley of Josaphat,* was a preacher's handbook for years. Blessed Ladislaus of Gielniow was known as "The Sun of the Polish Nation". Hugo de Digne was called "The Second Paul". Pope Alexander IV ordered the sermons of Gilbert of Tournai to be collected and edited for the use of future preachers. England had her John Forest, Ralph of Rosa, Haymo of Faversham; while it is easily demonstrable that the Franciscans, then newly reformed, preserved the Faith in Ireland against the so-called Reformation, by their preaching and example.

The moral nerves of the old and new worlds have reacted to the electric current of Franciscan preaching. If southern Europe had its Simon of Lipnica, John of Dukla and Pelbart, South America had its Francis Solanus and Mexico had her "Twelve Apostles". If the north of Europe had Berthold and John of Werden, the north of Asia had John of Monte Corvino, with his six suffragan bishops and preachers; and the north of Ireland its old, nameless Franciscan who kept the Faith alive in Donegal, and instructed the parents of him who filled for so many years in Armagh the See of Saint Patrick himself, the late Cardinal Logue.

If to follow the perennial influence of a man is a digression from his biography, then we have digressed; to us it seems rather that his influence is the better part of the man — the immortal part that makes of him a living tradition. Saint Francis entrusted to Anthony the task of inculcating in Franciscan pupils the spirit of Franciscan prayer and preaching. And Anthony, by word and example, carried out the command. The result was both quick and lasting. He himself became one of the mightiest preachers of the Middle Ages. In life he was a dynamic force in that Order which he embraced, in that country which he adopted. In death, his name and his immortal personality spread almost immediately through the world. The hidden beauty of the Franciscan spirit he made musically vocal, and the music was carried throughout Europe. Peter of Alcántara, Berthold of Ratisbon, Pelbart of Hungary — all of them preached what Francis had outlined and Anthony developed; they preached vice and virtue, punishment and glory, with brevity of speech, in concrete language that had its prototype in Judea and has had its continued fulfilment in the Franciscan pulpits of the world.

The masses of men and women respond whenever the message of the Gospel is given in words that they can understand and arguments that their untutored minds can grasp. Anthony often preached to crowds of thirty thousand people, and Franciscans of the following generations were not less attractive in their discourses. Francis preached to the birds; Anthony preached to the fishes: later, the Friars of the Middle Ages preached in the streets, in the market places, in cemeteries and on the village common.   People harkened and remembered; and remembering is one positive proof of a telling sermon. Little, the Franciscan historian, tells us, with point here, that one Robert Abovetheweye, of Ashby Mears, Northampton, remembered distinctly the sermon of a Friar after a lapse of twenty-one years; nay more, Robert fixed dates by that same sermon.

Such was the influence of the preaching begun by Saint Anthony.   It rang in converts wherever it was exercised; it changed not only men's hearts but actually the very architecture of their churches.   For Little, quoted above, adds this note: "Of no less importance were the sermons of the Friars in their own churches, for which a new form of architecture was evolved, suitable for holding the large congregations who came to hear the Word. Sermons were given, not only on Sundays and festivals, but on rainy days when the people took shelter in the Friars' churches."

To whom shall the glory go?   First to the gentle Seraph of Assisi who took men's broken hearts in his open hand and spoke to them direct, sincere words of comfort and cheer.   Next to that "glorious Franciscan spirit" which, through the centuries, noble men felt and heralded up and down the world.   And finally, and in large measure, to him who first translated so faithfully for heretic, peasant and apostate, the humble, holy spirit of Francis — to Saint Anthony of Padua, the first teacher of the Order, "The Hammer of Heretics", the "eldest son of Saint Francis"; to "Anthony our Bishop", the Wonder-worker of the whole world.

The Christ Child Appears to St. Anthony

C.B. Chambers

St. Anthony the Theologian

St. Anthony Lover of Solitude

C.B. Chambers

C.B. Chambers   St. Anthony In Meditation on the Mount

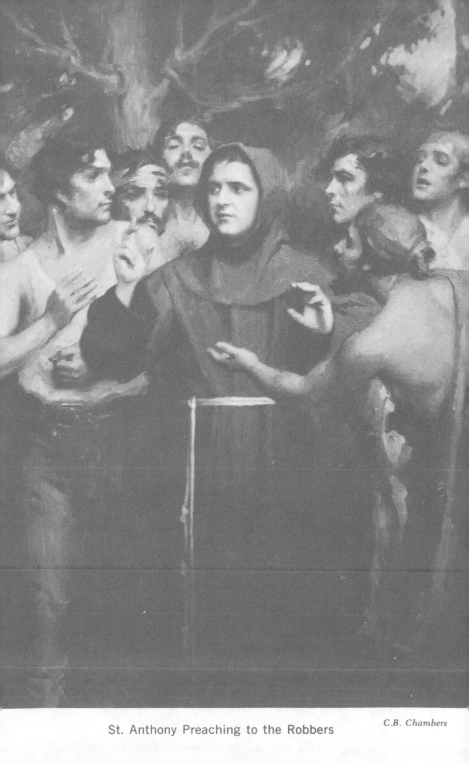

St. Anthony Preaching to the Robbers

C.B. Chambers

C.B. Chambers

St. Anthony a Priest

St. Anthony the Romanticist

C.B. Chambers

C.B. Chambers

St. Anthony and the Peasants

St. Anthony at Prayer

C.B. Chambers

C.B. Chambers

St. Anthony and the Christ Child

St. Anthony Fearless Apostle of Truth

C.B. Chambers

C.B. Chambers

St. Anthony Friend of Man

St. Anthony Friend in Need

C.B. Chambers

C.B. Chambers

St. Anthony Inspiration of Youth

St. Anthony Lover of Mary

C.B. Chambers

C.B. Chambers

St. Anthony Lover of the Poor

11

The Hammer of Heresy

L ANGUEDOC is a name with which to conjure. It brings memories of the boyhood of long ago, when we learned from our English grammar that *langue d'oc* and *langue d'oïl* represented two dialects of France. The one, *langue d'oïl*, belonged to the people of the north, where the Normans lived for a hundred and fifty years before marching on Hastings in 1066, thereafter changing the English language, and where the inhabitants said *oïl*, or *oui*, for "yes"; the other, *langue d'oc*, belonged to the south, where the inhabitants said *oc* for "yes". What visions we saw as the rhythmic word "Languedoc" rolled off our teacher's tongue! Visions of blue skies that bent over the snow and sunshine of the Pyrenees; of vineyards and orange-groves in the dew of early morning; of citron trees on the slopes that amplified the nightingale's note; of poplars that grew by the rumbling Garonne and the swelling Gironde. Visions of a land of sunshine and brightly colored dresses, of animals with panniers on their backs, of girls with coifs on their heads, of a people whose lives and thoughts ran to music. These it was that flitted distractingly between our boyish eyes and the much-marked pages of the book of English grammar, edited by one Alfred S. West, M. A., of Trinity College, Cambridge. And as we grew older we learned more names in southern France that held more music and musings — Carcassonne, Bergerac, Montpellier, Toulouse and Ariège and Limoges, Albi by the river Tarn, and Avignon on the Rhone.

It is true that we wandered at times into Gascony and threatened the borders of Aquitania; it is true that we were merely learning before a red-and-blue map on a white wall the names of towns in southern France. But when, in later years, history took a hand in our instruction, we discovered the value of the towns we had learned. History and geography began to interpret each other. We learned how Henry II of England, who was neither English nor Norman nor Saxon, but Angevin, invaded Ireland in 1171, even though he already had Anjou and Maine and Normandy and Poitou and Aquitania and Brittany across the sea; how he slew Thomas à Becket, and did penance at Canterbury, and made the family royal butlers by way of recompense — from whom, they say, came Anne Boleyn of later notoriety; how Henry was given a son and lost some of his foreign possessions; how Philip Augustus of France joined with this son of Henry, who is known to us as Richard the Lion-Hearted; how these two kings went on the Third Crusade and quarreled; how Philip returned to his English intrigues, and Richard was first imprisoned in Austria, and then mortally wounded at Limoges, seeking hidden treasure; how John Lackland quarreled with that great, cold intellect, Pope Innocent III, and was beaten by Innocent, and later by the nobles, and had to grant the Magna Charta on an island in the Thames; how Philip, because he was too busy with other plans, refused to wage war against the Albigenses, and left it to Simon de Montfort to oppose, with Pope Innocent's support, Raymond VI, Count of Toulouse, champion of heretics.

Such are a few of the memories from grammar-school and college days that come back as we reach the point in this short biography where Anthony goes across the Alps to convert the Albigenses of Albi by the river Tarn in Languedoc, in the year 1224. It was two years before the death of Saint Francis, and three years after the death of Saint Dominic, who had spent himself in that very province against those very heretics.

It was in September that Saint Francis sent Anthony to France — the same month in which, while kneeling amid the crags of La Verna, the Seraph of Assisi received the stigmata. We do not know if it was before or after there had been stamped on his flesh the Five Wounds of

Christ that Saint Francis bade the teacher Anthony go and carry on the work that his friend and brother Saint Dominic had laid down three years before. At any rate, he sent Anthony to Montpellier in Languedoc, with instructions to continue his lectures there to the Franciscan students, and to start, besides, a course of preaching against the Albigenses who were overturning southern France.

We have seen that the Albigenses were of the same kidney as the heretics in northern Italy. Both had, as the starting point of their teaching, the misconceived principle of a dual force, two gods in the world; both were religio-political, with their respective champions who opposed the pope. In Languedoc it was the counts of Toulouse who favored, sometimes openly, sometimes secretly, the fanatical sect. There was, besides, a large Jewish element in France which contributed to the confusion and rancor. Finally, the Albigenses were more in the order of a deadly secret society than were their cousins in Italy. They had a motto: Swear and forswear thyself, provided thou keep the secret. They had a slogan: Down with the Pope; down with the Catholic Church. They had a vice-regent, Bartholomew of Carcassonne. They had a head in Bulgaria with the title: The Servant of the Servants of the Holy Faith.

The Jews wanted possession of material things, and

to this end they played on the religious fanaticism of an
excited peasantry. This, in fact, was the core of the whole
tumor. The popes diagnosed it clearly from the first,
though for a long time they were unable to give it the
proper surgical treatment. The Fredericks of Germany
and the Philips of France and the Johns of England em-
barrassed rather than assisted them in the extermination
of this sect that would have robbed southern France and
northern Italy of faith and possessions.

As a matter of history, the possessions of the counts
of Toulouse *were* lost to them, and taken by the Crown
in 1229, after the disastrous war waged against them on
account of their heresy, by Simon de Montfort and Louis
VIII, Philip's son. It was in 1270, however, that the
whole country went to the Crown; and it was in this
same year that at the Council of Toulouse there was set
up for the first time, for the final extirpation of this East-
ern sect, what has been known since as the Inquisition.
The object of this institution was to drive from the soil
of France an enemy no less dangerous to the Catholic
faith than it was to the people of Languedoc.

Castile, Navarre and Aragon bordered Gascony and
Languedoc on the south. We must remember that at
this time cities were often self-governed under the
suzerainty of some king. Now Montpellier, to which
Anthony was sent, though in Languedoc, owed fealty to

the king of Aragon.   To understand this, we might suppose for a moment Connecticut to be one kingdom and
New Jersey another, with New Haven governing itself
independently of Connecticut and paying tithes to some
overlord in Trenton.   We could, to be realistic, set the
Rocky Mountain chain between them, calling it the
Pyrenees, and thus adding logic and clarity to the picture.

At any rate, since Montpellier was under Aragon, it
was staunchly Catholic; so much so that in 1224, the
year of Anthony's arrival, the French bishops convened
there in solemn council to deliberate plans for the
purpose of freeing southern France of her pests.   Raymond VII, the thankless ward of Innocent III, promised
his support.   He gave it waveringly.   Such was the situation in general as Anthony crossed the Alps and descended into the plains of France.   At the friary in Montpellier he carried on his course of lectures to the students
and finished his *Commentary on the Psalms* — a veritable
gold mine of biblical lore, and the basis, with the New
Testament, of most of his sermons.   For Anthony always
drew his inspiration from the Bible.   He preached the
Gospel from the Gospels, giving to every sentence in the
New Testament its Old Testament setting in prophecy
and history.

About 1225 he went to Toulouse to teach and preach
there.   The particular point of the controversy at this

time was centered on the Divinity of Christ — the dogma against which Manichaeism is directed, and the Albigensian heresy most particularly pointed. For instead of believing in one God and three Divine Persons, the Second of Whom is the Son of God, Who became incarnate, the Albigenses taught that a fallen power (that principle of evil already mentioned) was the creator and lord of the visible world.

The Church has had few men and fewer popular preachers as well fitted by study and natural powers of eloquence to prove the Divinity of Christ as was Anthony of Padua. He knew the Holy Scriptures by heart when scarcely more than a boy. He had spent his life pondering on the Gospels and on how their recorded life of Christ fulfills the prophecies of old. Moreover he was beginning, at this time, to exercise to the full that marvelous power of working miracles to substantiate his teaching which was given to him by God in such large measure.

Now, error of doctrine, even when its exponents are sincere, needs clever rhetoric to keep it alive in the hearts of the masses, but if these same masses can be shown that this erroneous doctrine is merely a blind to cover the stealthy activities of gross material greed, they soon forsake their deceivers. The Albigensian heresy, granting license and debauchery in the name of religion, stirring up the unlearned against the Church in the name of dogma, was thus merely using a decoy to lead the people astray so that its ringleaders, the secret sect, could enrich themselves from church property.

While Anthony's first task was to prove the Divinity of Christ, therefore, the actual condition of his success would consist in uncovering the real motives and ambitions of the Albigensian leaders. On the doctrine of the Divinity itself, there was not one of the opposite side who could oppose him intelligently. It is true that they had scattered very wrong teachings, had sown cockle while the husbandman was asleep; and no doubt the common people had gathered many wrong notions about Christ's nature, person and mission. But it would be child's play for Anthony to correct this type of error, if only these people would come to him and listen.

He was lucky in this; for his natural eloquence drew thousands. First laying before them the arguments for Christ's Divinity, he came to the practical point of his work by challenging the teachers and preachers of Manichaeism to public debate to defend their doctrine. None answered. He then pointed out to the people the weakness, the hypocrisy, the deceit, of their leaders, and their real motive, namely, greed for gold. He showed his hearers how their own unchecked desire for license had been used to rob them of their faith and property.

Anthony held a trump hand: he played every card effectively. The scales fell from the eyes of the people. To quote the words of Wadding: "The heretics and the very abettors of Manichaeism returned in numbers to the Catholic Faith." The bishop was overcome at the Friar Preacher's success. And it was when these sinners returned that Anthony showed most clearly the gentle spirit of the true pastor of souls, the spirit that is so much of Saint Francis of Assisi. We should have preferred it here if historians had been a little more exact in their terminology when recording this chapter of Anthony's life, and had given him the real title that he earned in Toulouse, namely, "The Hammer of Heresy" rather than "The Hammer of Heretics". For when these returned, he reproached them not. It was his task to show them the real character of this Christ Whom he preached. He merely taught them anew the love and mercy of Him Whom they had been led to deny. He merely told them again of Christ's forgiveness of sinners; he merely restored to them the old, comforting religion that they had learned from their parents in childhood.

12

The Worker of Wonders

"**I**F THERE is anything more impossible than a miracle, it is its impossibility. And if there is anything more indiscernible than a miracle, it is the reason why people call it indiscernible. This to a man of mere common sense, who also believes in a God Almighty and All-wise. To such a man there is something pleasingly absurd in the spectacle of a creature drawing up a Magna Charta for the limitation of his Creator's power, and when he has done so, refusing to believe his senses when God oversteps his man-made boundaries. For a man of common sense generally has a sense of humor; and a sense of humor is a short cut to humility, as the sense of the ridiculous is to the sense of the miraculous" (Arthur Little, S. J., M. A., in *Studies,* March, 1931).

This author has such clear-cut, up-to-date statements on the matter of miracles that we will copy verbatim his definition, and some of the subjoined remarks. He asks:

"What is a miracle? I define it as a work perceptible to the senses, which either in itself or in its manner surpasses all the powers of the material universe, and to which God positively consents." Again: "Mere man can do what mere man has done. . . . No assumption of luck, or of genius, or of psychic force (the three ways some one or all of which would have to be used to produce a miracle by natural means) in the wonder-worker will serve to subvert this principle, for each of these belongs in some measure to many other men. Human nature is a constant thing, and its powers only vary within certain limits."

This short apology for the possibility of miracles is perhaps not amiss in this enlightened day when we have a tendency to ask for the formula, the mathematics, of every act, high and low. Science has explained so much that some have come to think it can explain all. And when science itself runs headlong into a miracle it is not overgracious to its rival; it has a tendency to curl its lips and, like a boastful boy, to assert that it could have done that too if it had been there, or at least could have detected the trick. The first point is, of course, that science was not there, that is, our twentieth-century conception of science; the second point is that the miracle was worked even without it.

To sit in a room in New York and have one's voice reproduced in London — that is science. To be preaching in a church in New York and, at the same instant, to be present and chanting in one's own voice a psalm in a monastery in London — that is a miracle. To put a man to death with an invisible current we call electricity is science; to raise a man from the dead by an invisible cooperation with the Author of life is a miracle. And we are quite as certain of miracles as we are of science. We are quite as justified in believing men of the first or thirteenth century, when they tell us a man was raised to life, as we are in believing men of the twentieth century when they tell us a man was put to death. There is this difference, however, and it is not flattering to our age: we might very easily see a man being killed in the twentieth century; we do not know where we could go to see one being brought back from the dead. But had we lived in the days of Christ, or in the days of Anthony of Padua, we could have seen this very miracle being worked. Others saw it; and we can find no justifiable reason for doubting their sanity, their sincerity or their sense. They spoke of what they saw, and they were not dupes. Twenty centuries from now it will be wronging our honesty and insulting our intelligence for men of that day to laugh at the facts that we have recorded in this.

If we have come to doubt miracles, the loss is ours. Demanding to see too much, we have come to see less. We have said that science, and a broad, hazy, ill-defined factor called nature, are answerable for all things; in consequence we are left within the range of the so-called wonders produced by these two factors.

"Mere man can do what mere man has done." *We* can ascend into the air in machines. That is no miracle; the miracle is that men were not able to do that two thousand years ago, or more if you wish. The ignorance of man for five thousand odd years of the forces beneath his hand, is the nearest approach to a miracle that we can find in modern inventions. Why should man boast today of doing a thing that his ancestors of forty hundred generations ago could and should have done? To ascend into the thin air without any machine, or natural or scientific appendage, that is a miracle; and the saints did it centuries ago. Sensible, prosaic people saw them and recorded it; and just because we can ascend in an airplane, why should we laugh loudly at those who say they saw a man ascending without one? Why deny the supernatural because we have found out a few more things about the natural?

We should look with excusable astonishment at an erstwhile common, plodding and trustworthy citizen who, suddenly, and without the slightest warning whatever, burst into the headlines of the evening paper with the "discovery" that grass grows and that water runs downhill. Our astonishment would turn to concern if he announced, in a follow-up story, that because of these two

natural phenomena which had suddenly come to his knowledge he had decided to give up all belief in a Supreme
Being, to set his face in derision against all religion, to
treat for the future with like contempt his former notions
of the sanctity of marriage, the spiritual ties of the family,
the saving influence of moral training, and in general,
because of the green condition of his lawn, to break
away from all convention and tradition. We might be
pardoned for not comprehending clearly the connection
between grass growing and a man's departure from the
tenets of civilization.

The case seems far-fetched; but why should we, today,
laugh at all supernatural things simply because we have
made the marvelous discovery that gasoline explodes, and
that the air offers resistance to a propeller? The marvel
would be if someone could keep gasoline from exploding
under its ordinary conditions for exploding. Did we
create gasoline or air or electricity or grass or water?
We know that we did not, but that a Creator put them
there beneath our hand. And as soon as we discovered
them, simply because we did so, we denied the existence
of the Supreme Being Who put them there. Such is the
havoc that pseudo-science has wrought in logic and common sense.

All our discoveries in the natural order have merely
moved us along a few inches in the same flat line of

things natural. Though we possessed all the scientific lore
of the day, we might stand before a water-pot full of water
till death did us part, calling on the water in the name of
science to become wine — and it would remain water.
If rain were falling, we might exhort it with all our natural
eloquence not to fall on a certain field; and at the end, that
field would be as wet as those surrounding it. Yet Christ
by a divine act of His Will changed water into wine;
Anthony of Padua, at Brive in France, by the power
given him by God, kept a servant dry in the midst of a
downpour.

To men and women of faith there is nothing strange
in these things, of course; for they know that God has
always vouchsafed to His servants the power of working
miracles when His external glory and the salvation of
souls call for miracles. They know that God has not
asked Himself how following generations, simply because they have plodded their way into a knowledge of
electricity, will regard these supernatural actions.   And
if southern France in the beginning of the thirteenth
century, God's glory, the life of His Church in that locality and the salvation of souls, needed a man gifted
with this power from heaven, southern France got such
a man, one who stands above all other mere men in history as a worker of wonders.

We have said that on Anthony's entrance into France

there began the fruitful time of miracles. We know that it did not end with his leaving France, or even with his leaving this earth, but has continued to the present day.

There are, says Roger Maloney, O. F. M., in the *Franciscan Almanac* for 1931, some "fifty laboriously sifted and well authenticated miracles recorded by the Bollandists." We can mention only a few of them. We shall commence with an incident that is not a miracle in the sense of implying Anthony's exercise of any supernatural power, but that shows rather his close relationship to Heaven, his tender love for Mary, the Queen of Heaven, his devotion to her at whose request Christ performed, at the wedding feast of Cana in Galilee, the first miracle of His public life. We shall relate it in the words of Father Léopold de Chérancé, O. S. F. C., to whom we are indebted both for information and inspiration in this little work:

"It was on the 14th of August when, in the Convent at Toulouse, at the office of Prime, the Friars were wont to read the lesson from the Martyrology for the Feast on the following day. The Martyrology then in general use in France was that of Usuard, who, in reference to the beautiful festival of the morrow, made these remarks: As yet the Church has given no decision upon the bodily Assumption of the Blessed Virgin, exercising a prudent reserve as to trivial or apocryphal legends.' To treat as an apocryphal legend a truth so certain and so constantly affirmed by tradition, deeply wounded the heart of the faithful servant of Mary. Hence when the bell rang for Prime, he was greatly perplexed and agitated as to what course to take. To absent himself from the choir, without any further reason, was an infraction of the Rule; to be present and listen to that equivocal statement of Usuard was equivalent to giving a tacit assent to that against which his heart protested. Our Blessed Lady herself deigned to console her faithful servant, who had so often published her greatness and defended the prerogatives which flow from her Divine Motherhood. She appeared to him in all the splendor of her beauty, surrounded by a dazzling light. With his bodily eyes he gazed upon her who outshines the stars, who is purer than crystal, and more unspotted than the virgin snow on the mountain tops. He heard the voice whose celestial harmony ravishes the ears of the Angels and the Blessed; Mary's words were: 'Be assured, my son, that this body of mine, which has been the living Ark of the Word Incarnate, has been preserved from the corruption of the grave. Be equally assured that, three days after my death, it was carried upon the wings of Angels to the right hand of the Son of God, where I reign as Queen.' Each word, as it fell from the august lips of the Queen of Heaven, filled his mind with wondrous light and his heart with unspeakable joy. When she disappeared it seemed to him as if all the delights of Paradise had flooded his soul, yet was it but one drop of bliss from the cup of happiness that inebriates the elect.

"He understood, however, that this apparition was not a mere personal favor. He spoke of it boldly, bearing witness to the truth; he became the champion and the apostle of the glorious mystery of Mary's Assumption, as the Patriarch of Assisi had been of her Immaculate Conception. Inspired by his fervor he gave utterance to the beautiful versicle which has been incorporated in her office on the Assumption: 'The august Mother of God has been assumed into Heaven, and placed above the angelic choirs.'

"On the day when the Church defines this truth, when she will call forth from their tombs the faithful servants and champions of Mary to bear testimony to the universal and constant belief, she will cite amongst her foremost witnesses Saint Anthony of Padua."

Anthony's stay in Toulouse was short, as he was made superior at Puy-en-Velay in September, 1225 — one year after he had arrived in France. Two incidents that happened at this time show his gift of prophecy. A lady of the district came to him and asked for his prayers in her coming trial of maternity. Anthony promised them, and foretold that a son would be born to her who would become a Franciscan and later win the martyr's palm.

It happened as he said.   Philip was the Friar's name; and he was put to death by the Saracens at Azot.   He asked that he be martyred last so that he might encourage his companions.   After undergoing fearful tortures for his zeal, he was finally beheaded.

The second incident reminds us quickly that Anthony is still in the land of heretics and fanatics.   In Puy lived a certain notary, a great heretic and a greater debauchee. He hated the Church and all her ministers wholeheartedly, to begin with, and Anthony was but a short time in town before he hated him particularly; for every time they chanced to meet, Anthony removed his "soli Deo" to the rake.   Seeing nothing but mockery in this — and indeed it is hard to blame him for thus interpreting this token of veneration from a saint — the notary one day stopped Anthony after he had saluted him in the customary way, exclaiming that only fear of God's instantaneous wrath stayed his hand from running him through with the sword for such public mockery.

"I would gladly endure martyrdom for the love of God," said Anthony, "but such is not His will.   But it is revealed to me that one day you will be an illustrious martyr.   When that time comes I beg you to remember me."

The prophecy was fulfilled in this way: The Bishop of Puy, Stephen III, organized a local crusade against the Saracens, and the notary, moved by grace, or moved by something, went with them.   But even grace does not uproot a man's natural temperament; and among the Turks the notary from Puy-en-Velay was as energetic and fearlessly zealous for Christ as at home he had been openly hostile to His ministers.   When the Bishop preached gently to the Saracens, the notary arose and told his lordship that such speech was far too moderate for such people.   The Bishop quieted him, and he listened discontentedly for some time longer.   Finally, unable to contain himself, he got up to show the Bishop and the bystanders how Turks should be spoken to.   With fiery eloquence he informed them that Christ was the only Son of God, and that Mohammed, their prophet, was merely a hypocrite, an impostor and an emissary of Satan.   The Turks soon stopped this flow of theological rhetoric.   He was torn away and handed over to three days of torture. And as he went to his death, he suddenly remembered what Anthony had told him, and rejoiced that he had won martyrdom so easily.

Among the characteristics of the saints, fearlessness is marked.   It was present in John the Baptist, confronting Herod with his sin.   It was present in Saint Paul, and after Pentecost it was not absent in Saint Peter.   Saint Francis had it in a marked degree, and Anthony was not without it, as we shall see specifically in a later chapter.

For the present we shall notice that on being invited to preach before a senate in Bourges, two months after his arrival in Velay, he openly and in the presence of Bishops, Archbishops and Cardinal de St. Ange, solemnly assembled, rebuked the Archbishop for allowing certain matters under his jurisdiction to go unnoticed. But Simon de Sully, the Archbishop, the confidant of Pope Honorius III and Saint Louis of France, was not to be outdone in moral bravery. He threw himself at the Friar's feet and begged the pardon of all for his negligence in the duties committed to his care.

At Bourges, too, Anthony held with Guillard the Jew a discussion on the Real Presence of Christ in the Eucharist. Guillard, a ringleader in the secret sect of the Albigensians and a bitter enemy of the Church, had come out of curiosity to hear Anthony preach. The sermon annoyed his conscience without convincing his mind. Later the two men met, probably by accident, and entered into an argument regarding Christ's presence in the tabernacle. Anthony asked this question: "How is it that while the Turk believes the word of Mohammed, the philosopher the word of Aristotle, you, who boast of being such a true Israelite, refuse to believe the word of your God made man?"

Here follows, in most lives of Saint Anthony, a discussion regarding the miracle in which the mule adored

the Blessed Sacrament. Little fruit is gained from it;
and we can let it pass with the remark that perhaps Anthony duplicated at Bourges the wonder he had wrought
at Rimini. At any rate Guillard was converted; and is
said to have erected a church on the spot where the meeting had taken place.

Anthony continued his labors in this locality till September, 1226, when the Provincial Chapter was held. On
the Feast of the Exaltation of the Holy Cross, he was
invited to preach to the brethren. He did so, and took
for his text: "Jesus of Nazareth, King of the Jews."
While he was preaching this sermon, Saint Francis, who
at this time was living at the bishop's house in Assisi,
appeared to Brother Monaldo in Anthony's audience at
Arles, smiled on the brethren with radiant face, and
blessed them with his wounded, outstretched hands. It
was nineteen days before Saint Francis' death. At this
Chapter Anthony was made Custos of Limoges.

Political events in southern France were hurrying on:
Louis VIII had marched against the Albigenses, had
taken Lyons and Avignon; and was pressing on through
the falling leaves of these autumn months, toward Toulouse and his own death — which took place on No-
vember 8, 1226.

Anthony came to Limoges to assume his duties in this
same month. Immediately on his arrival, he preached

to a host of people in the Cemetery of St. Paul. He
was the guest of the Benedictines of the Abbey of St.
Martin; and on the following day he preached in the
abbey itself. The Benedictines, profoundly impressed
with both sermons, have left us the texts which Anthony
developed. In a recent chapter we spoke at length on
Anthony's method of preaching. It was in fact by this
means that he won all hearts to God and to himself. He
expounded always the allegorical meaning of the Bible,
drawing copiously from the facts of natural history to
illustrate his reflections on the yearnings, the destiny and
the sublimity of the human soul. Another point which
gave him distinction was that his own words were so
interlaced with biblical quotations, and so penetrated by
his deep knowledge of both Testaments. We give here
a portion of the sermon Anthony preached on this occasion to the Benedictines of St. Martin. Its topic was
the beauties of the monastic life:

" 'Who will give me the wings of a dove and I will
fly and be at rest?' Such is the cry of a soul that is weary
of this world and longs for the solitude and peace of the
cloistered life. It is of the religious life that the Prophet
Jeremias spoke when he said: 'Leave the cities, ye that
dwell in Moab, and dwell in the rock: and be ye like the
dove that maketh her nest in the mouth of the hole in the
highest place.' 'Leave the cities,' that is, the sins and

vices which dishonor, the tumult which prevents the soul from raising herself to God, and often from thinking of Him. Leave the cities, for it is written: 'I have seen iniquity and contradiction in the city. Day and night shall iniquity surround it upon its walls: and in the midst thereof are labor and injustice. And usury and deceits have not departed from its streets.' There is to be found iniquity against God and man: contradiction against the preacher of truth; labor in the ambitious cares of the world: injustice in its dealings; knavery and usury in its business transactions. 'Ye that dwell in Moab,' that is, in the world which is seated in pride as the city of Moab. All is pride in the world: pride of the intellect, which refuses to humble itself before God; pride of the will, which refuses to submit to the will of God; pride of the senses, which rebel against reason and dominate it . . . .

"But to leave the world, to live remote from the tumult of cities, to keep oneself unspotted from their vices, is not sufficient for the religious soul. Hence the Prophet adds: 'Dwell in the rock.' Now this rock is Jesus Christ. Establish yourself in Him: let Him be the constant theme of your thoughts, the object of your affections. Jacob reposed upon a stone in the wilderness, and while he slept he saw the heavens opened and conversed with Angels, receiving a blessing from the Lord. Thus will it be with those who place their entire trust in Jesus Christ. They will be favored with heavenly visions; they will live in the company of Angels, they will be blessed as Jacob was, 'to the north and south, to the east and west.' To the north, which is the Divine breath mortifying the flesh and its concupiscences; to the east, which is the light of faith and the merit of good works; to the south, which is the full meridian splendor of wisdom and charity; to the west, which is the burial of the old man with his vices. But as to the soul which does not repose upon this rock, it cannot expect to be blessed by the Lord.

" 'And be ye like the dove that maketh her nest in the mouth of the hole of the highest place.' If Jesus Christ is the rock, the hole of the rock, in which the religious soul is to seek shelter and take up her abode, is the wound in the side of Jesus Christ. This is the safe harbor of refuge, to which the Divine Spouse calls the religious soul when He speaks to her in the words of the Canticle, 'Arise, my love, my beautiful one, and come, O my dove, that art in the clefts of the rock, in the deep hollow of the wall.' The Divine Spouse speaks of the numberless clefts of the rock, but He also speaks of the deep hollow. There were, indeed, in His Body numberless wounds, and one deep wound in His Side; this leads to His Heart, and it is hither He calls the soul He has espoused. To her He extends His Arms; to her He opens wide His Sacred Side and Divine Heart, that she may come and hide therein.   By retiring into the clefts of the rock the dove is safe from the pursuit of birds of prey, and, at the same time, she prepares for herself a quiet refuge where she may calmly repose and coo in peace.   So the religious soul finds in the Heart of Jesus a secure refuge against the wiles and attacks of Satan, and a delightful retreat.

"However, we must not rest merely at the entrance to the hole in the rock, we must penetrate its depths.   At the mouth of the deep hollow, at the mouth of the wound in His Side, we shall indeed find the Precious Blood which has redeemed us.   This Blood pleads for us and demands mercy for us.   But the religious soul must not stay at the entrance.   When she has heard and understood the Voice of the Divine Blood, she must hasten to the very source from which it springs, into the very innermost sanctuary of the Heart of Jesus.   There she will find light, peace and ineffable consolations.   'And be ye like the dove that maketh her nest in the deep hollow of the rock.'   The dove builds her nest with little pieces of straw she gathers up here and there.   And how are we to build up an abode in the Heart of Jesus?   This Divine Saviour, Who so mercifully gives us the place wherein we are to make our abode, furnishes us at the same time with the materials wherewith to construct it.   O religious soul, dove beloved of Christ, behold those little pieces of straw which the world tramples under its feet.   They are the virtues practised by thy Saviour and thy Spouse, of which He Himself has set thee an example: humility, meekness, poverty, penance, patience and mortification. The world despises them as useless pieces of straw; nevertheless, they will be for thee the material wherewith to construct thy dwelling place forever, in the profound hollow of the rock, in the Heart of Jesus."

Here we have the soul and the genius of Anthony: a torrent of thoughts tumbling in revivifying eloquence on the minds of all his hearers. At Limoges his fame continued to grow and expand into that crescendo of glory which finally swept across all national boundaries and reverberated through the world. Heretics were converted; the good grew in virtue. He continued to work miracles in increasing numbers. In his own convent he reads the heart of a novice who is about to quit the Order secretly, and strengthens him in his vocation. In the square in Limoges his word "binds up the rain in the clouds," so that his multitudes of hearers remain dry in the midst of a tempest. At St. Junien he truly foretells that the platform from which he intends to preach will collapse, but that no one will be injured. A penitent's sins disappear from the paper on which he had written them as he reads them to Saint Anthony in confession. A woman, in her eagerness to hear him, confuses her child's bath with a tub of boiling water, and returns to find it splashing about unharmed in the steaming vessel. Another mother, finding her baby dead, hurries to Anthony with her grief. He consoles her and bids her return home, where she discovers the child playing with his toys.

We might continue the list indefinitely, but with one more we shall stop. We have left it to the last, for it is that miracle in which art and poetry have immortalized Anthony of Padua. Consoler as he ever was of others, preacher as he ever was of the mercies of God, the Son of God Himself came to console His servant, the humble, holy Anthony. And he came not in agony or in complaint, but as he had come to Mary on Christmas morning when the Angels filled the sky with music, and shepherds and their sheep looked up from the lowly earth and saw the Saviour in the form of a child. Perhaps it was Mary herself, she whom Anthony loved so tenderly, who brought her Infant from the skies and set Him in Anthony's arms. However, in an old castle in France he began that intimate union with the Infant Jesus which now for seven hundred years he has enjoyed in heaven; began to learn anew the exquisite tenderness of that Infant Heart for mankind which for seven hundred years he has brought so punctually to man's assistance.

To tell the story fittingly let us borrow from Father de Chérancé:

"One evening he sought the hospitality of the Lord of Châteauneuf, who, in the words of a Limousin chronicler, 'had a particular attachment for him and his Order.' Having retired to his room, he as usual prolonged his prayerful vigil far into the night. Suddenly he found himself surrounded by a supernatural brightness, more brilliant than the sun in its splendor, amidst which the Lover of humble souls appeared to him, not crowned with thorns and with bleeding temples, but under the form of a little Child of marvelous beauty and grace. O the bliss of that hour! It is impossible to describe the emotion that thrilled the frame of Anthony at the sight of his God under an appearance so divinely sweet, the joy that filled his soul as he pressed his heart against that of his Lord and felt its throbbing. The secrets of the great King are too sublime for translation into mortal language, they must be left untold. All we know is that, before ascending to His throne of glory, the Divine Child lavished on His favored servant caresses that might have excited the jealousy of Angels, were they capable of feeling envy; caresses only to be understood by those who know the infinite delicacy of Eternal Love. By a special permission of Providence for the glory of the faithful Saint, the Lord of Châteauneuf, attracted by the extraordinary light which filled his house, saw the vision with his own eyes. Anxious to learn what had passed, he asked Saint Anthony, who, knowing that his host had been a witness of the high mystery which had taken place in his castle, consented, in so far as it concerned him, to tell him what had passed, conditionally upon his promising not to reveal it during his — Anthony's — life.

"After Anthony's death his friend revealed the secret which he had, according to his promise, guarded faithfully until then, and sealed his statement by oath."

Now and then, in the chapters that follow, we shall have occasion to mention Anthony in the light of a workers of miracles; but while he lived, France has the distinction of having written his sojourn there exclusively in terms of miracles. And in this matter France is very much like each of us individually; for has not his whole relationship to us been calendared by acts of kindness that amount to miracles? Have we not known him best in those agonizing moments when we needed him most? Would we have known him half so well had we not needed him so much? Torn and bleeding France needed him; our own uprooted hopes and longings have often called to him as loudly as did the wounds of Languedoc and Limousin. And he has been to each one of us, since we besought him first, what he has been to men and women through the ages.

Has not each of us, countless times, seen enacted before Saint Anthony's shrine in the shadowy corner of a church, the little drama which told its story of hope and love and fear, and a fine faith that conquered? Have we not seen help sought and obtained there, and gratitude freely spring from a bursting heart? Before his statue we have seen a mother kneel in anguish and plead for things of which only a mother's heart can know; kneel and implore help in those things which only a mother's soul can fear. We have seen the gray-haired merchant bend in quiet agony, and ask that at least his good name and his business honor be left him from the wreck of his life's work. We have seen a young man and woman kneel in the flower-perfumed darkness of a June night and pray for strength for each other.

Back through the centuries that ended before our own brief life began, Saint Anthony has been looking down on the world's poor and suffering, on the upturned faces that are prematurely old, on the humbled heads that are gray before their time under the blighting touch of disappointment and sorrow. Through the flight of years, while the fortunes and boundaries of nations changed, while names appeared for a moment above the sea of history, then fell back into its dark waters to be forgotten, Saint Anthony has pressed the Divine Infant closer to his heart, and has stretched out his hand to bless, to comfort, to help the prostrate millions at his feet. Through the divine institution we call the Communion of Saints, the crushed and beaten of the world go to this young Saint for that hearing which their fellows have denied them. He speaks to the Infant in his arms in a prayer that has no words; and the casements of heaven open, and light and strength and eager love come earthward to heal the broken hearts of men.

In this group which we may see in our churches— Saint Anthony, with the Christ-Child in his arms and a supplicant at his feet — we have that trinity of power, pity and need, that interflowing of supplication, sorrow and balm, of love and gratitude, which are the true, and indeed the only, meaning of religion. Many a sorrow-laden man owes it that he is stamped with the veritable image of God's own Son in His agony and God's own saints in their martyrdom, to the winning appeal and supernatural compassion of our Saint.

Our heavenly Father ordained that we should be helped in our major trials; that we should go to Him through our intercessors. It is as useless as it is tiresome to invent other courses — to tell men and women to become modern, free, confident of a source of independent strength within themselves. There is nothing modern in a mistake. It is enormously flattering, but tragically unfair, to tell man that he has the powers of God within his subliminal self. It is a waste of time to repeat a formula that is intrinsically inadequate to bring him to the receding and enclouded portals of happiness. I may say to myself from the cradle to the grave, "I will be strong. I will be successful. I will be confident. I will be independent and self-sufficient. I am the godly carver of my own destiny." I may say these things over and over, with the monotonous repetition of a weed dipping into a stream; and they will be about as efficacious in shaping my life as are the light strokes of the weed in turning the course of the river. It will be with my formula as it generally is with the weed: some day the stream of events will become a torrent, and tear my set phrases from their thin roots. God is not to be banished from His world by any subjective nonsense of man. He has stood the test of the ages as man's Father, and our greatest wisdom is in going to Him through His saints.

It has been so with others, it is not different with us. For though we are of a sophisticated age, we are not the first creation of the Almighty. It is not our office to find substitutes for God and religion and spiritual intercession and heavenly help. Not only is the project impossible. The idea is insane. To throw religion and the comforts of intercessory prayer overboard, is to jettison our last supply of fresh water and wet our swollen lips with the briny tide.

In the pains and heartbreaks that crush us most our fellow-man is unable to help us, for he is feeling the same

anguish.   Though it causes us a pang when we discover
this, it marks a great advance for our souls.   Only when
there is no creature on the horizon of our sorrow to
whom we can appeal, do we go to our heavenly Father
Who awaits us.   Then we run to Him as children who
have lost their way in a wood; or as gaunt, tattered men
who have been tossed for days on an uncharted sea.
Man turns to God only when, by an act of his soul, he
sees no one but God, just as the needle finds the pole
only when it is insulated from local attractions.

So it is the influence, or power, or creature, or saint,
which brings us most directly to God that will receive
our fullest measure of gratitude.   Herein, precisely, lies
the mystery of the deep love and devotion for Saint
Anthony among men; for no other saint in the calendar
so consistently and eternally offers God to man — and
God in His most loving and lovable form.   He early
realized that when man prays, the only answer is God
Himself, in the very form in which He came on earth
to answer men's prayers.

Though perhaps mankind in the mass has not reasoned
it out thus, the multitude has been quick in its instinct
of gratitude toward Saint Anthony.   Through all the
ephemeral glory that seven hundred years have given and
taken away from men, his fame has steadily increased.
The sun has touched to brightness many times the bee-

tling headlands of Portugal, and each morning its rays have gilded to new brilliance the halo of him who sleeps in Padua.   Men and women in rags and in purple, in hunger that is of the heart, in sorrow and desolation; men and women carrying on their bent backs the full pack of human woe, have crept to the statue of this boyish Saint. Gratitude that breaks the heart and makes every fragment eloquent, has given to Saint Anthony of Padua his meed of fame.   He who in life loved the cloistered quiet, has crossed national boundaries and wide seas; with the Christ-Child in his arms he has answered the prayers of ages and nations, and is, in consequence, hailed as the "Saint of the whole world" — worker of miracles, even the miracle of making us understand.

13

To Rome,
to Rimini, to Padua

SAINT ANTHONY'S life might almost be called miraculous judged from the viewpoint of mere activity. Even in our day of world-wide advertising, for a man in his thirtieth year to be universally renowned is accounted grounds enough for naming public parks and highways after him, or for striking his features on congressional medals. So even the incredulous of our age ought not to hesitate to give Anthony of the thirteenth century that share of honor for public service which they would rush onto a platform to accord a man of the twentieth. For by the time Anthony was thirty he had mastered the science of his day in what would now be a combination of all our university courses; had traversed the Mediterranean, traveled up Italy on foot, and been personally appointed by the greatest man of the thirteenth century the first teacher of a tremendous Order; had preached, lectured and traveled through northern Italy, crossed the Alps, gone on foot through southern France, preached to huge concourses there, worked innumerable miracles, helped to stabilize legitimate government, and spoken before national synods.

And now we shall see how, departing from France, by land or water we know not, for Italy, Anthony came, by what route we know not, to Rome the Eternal.

Though Saint Dominic had labored against the Albigenses, he had died without seeing the heresy stamped out in Languedoc. And though Anthony preached there, wrought miracles, won scores back to the Faith, he left France on this Romeward journey without seeing the sect as a whole converted. But for all of that, Dominic had given the heresy its first mortal wound; and Anthony had dealt the blow which hastened its end.

We have seen that though Louis VIII died in 1226, as he was attacking Toulouse, it was in that year, and through his activities and those of Simon de Montfort, that the power of the counts of Toulouse was broken. Louis IX (Saint Louis), opposed by the nobles who wanted feudalism to endure, supported by the pope, and advised by that prudent woman, Blanche of Castile, his mother, took the throne at Rheims, in 1226. He was then only eleven, so that it was during the regency of Blanche that a treaty was made, in 1229, with Raymond VII, Count of Toulouse. In 1237, by a clever stroke due either to romance or to politics, Jeanne of Toulouse was married to the King's brother, Alphonse of Poitiers.

This marriage strengthened the treaty which, in fact, finally led to the complete absorption of the south by the Crown, and deprived the Albigenses of a political leader. Thus, ten years after Anthony's departure from France, the Albigensian heresy moldered into ashes and dust — sodden reminders of a reign of fire and blood.

As we have noted before, Saint Francis died in the October of 1226. The news, together with an announcement of a General Chapter for May 30 of the following year, was sent to the brethren by Elias, who governed in the meantime. We have already studied the character of Elias at length. Now that Francis was dead, this man of course had supporters and opponents amongst the Friars. Some wished him to succeed Francis; others fought with might and main against the movement. It is sometimes said that Saint Anthony was appointed to go to Rome at this time to consult with the pope on the possibility of uniting the factions and electing Elias as Minister General. This may or may not have been the motive of Anthony's journey; but it seems established that it was toward the end of 1226 that he quitted Limoges for Rome. Gregory IX ascended the Papal Throne on March 19, 1227. He had been that Cardinal Ugolino of Ostia, the friend, admirer and official adviser of Saint Francis. A tangled chapter of Franciscan history regarding changes in the Rule of the Order begins with this date, which, not being pertinent to our purpose, it is not our task to unravel.

Of course Gregory IX had often heard of Anthony, his eloquence and his power of working miracles. The story goes that as soon as he arrived in Rome the Pope commissioned him to preach to the people. Holy Week was ending, and the pageant and ritual that had filled Rome during the conclave was hushed now for the solemn services of the last three days of Lent. The nobles and church dignitaries who had come to Rome for the papal coronation filled the streets with their retinues and their purple glory.

Anthony's desire had been to remain unknown in the city, and to replenish his soul with meditation in the great basilicas and at the tombs of the martyrs. But just as at Forlì he had mounted the pulpit at the command of his superior, so now he responded to the invitation of the Pope to speak on the real meaning of the great Gospel story the Church was celebrating.

Men and women from every corner of Europe were there to listen, for the preacher's fame was known to all. And on this occasion, as on another when He had come to the aid of Saint Peter, the Holy Ghost gave Anthony the gift of tongues; for everyone in that heterogeneous throng heard the Saint speak in his native language.

Before this event and after it Anthony had marvelous

success as a preacher; but there is, in this picture of the
Holy Week sermon in Rome, something of unique significance, beauty and strength.   At Anthony's feet sits the
gray-haired Pontiff, native kindliness and strong faith
meeting in his mien; around and behind his august person range the Cardinals who have just elected him to the
See of Peter.   The nobles, their decorations laid aside in
honor of Him Who on these days was stripped of His
seamless garment, form wing guards; and behind these
stand and kneel Frank and Slav and Greek, German and
Briton and men of the Latin race.   The Holy Spirit Who
had come in a special manner to preside over the earlier
conclave, still lingers in holy brooding over the vast as-
semblage. Before them stands a Friar still in his
early manhood. His face is pale from fasting; but
the pallor lends brilliancy to the eye which flashes with
genius as the message of the Passion rushes from his lips.
Moses and the Prophets, the Evangelists and Fathers of
the Church — all that inspiration, revelation and deep
reflection have to tell about Him Who was crucified —
are fused in the utterance of this young man in a convic-
tion and a plea profound, piercing and touched with
unearthly power.   The lines of his brown robe follow
his movement as he sways to the mighty pulse of inspiration. His white cord falls to his sandaled feet.   His
tonsured head carries around it a circle of light.

When Saint Anthony had finished preaching on this occasion, men rose up, went to their homes and took scourges in their hands to purify their lives. Pope Gregory, in the presence of all, pronounced the young Friar to be the living "Ark of the Testament". But though Anthony has reached the summit of fame, his heart is humble within him; and when the Pope presses him to remain in the Pontifical Court, he pleads instead to be allowed to retire to the silence of the Italian hills. He goes into solitude for a time in that land which he is not destined to leave again until his soul goes home to Paradise, and the inhabitants of Padua, out of frenzied love for him, contend for the possession of his body.

At the General Chapter of 1227, by common opinion, Saint Anthony was made Provincial of the province of Bologna. Be this as it may, he carried on his missions through northern Italy. The Guelphs and Ghibellines still opposed each other; many of the cities had proclaimed their independence, looking to Pope or to Emperor, as the case might be, to protect their claims. It was Italy's War of the Roses. City contended against city. Pisa destroyed Amalfi. Genoa ruined Pisa. Venice fought with Genoa for the control of the sea.

Florence was Guelphic, but this was not enough for her: two other factions, the Blacks and the Whites, had arisen within her gates. The Blacks were Guelphs. The

Whites became Ghibellines. The student of history will recall that, a little after the time of our story, Pope Boniface VIII brought into Italy Charles of Valois, who gave the Guelphs supremacy in Florence; after which Henry VII entered Italy, and partially restored imperialism to the Ghibellines. Avignon and the Babylonian Exile followed in the steps of the Angevins and the Valois.

To return to Anthony: at the request of John Parenti, the Minister General, a Florentine, he preached in the city on the Arno during the Advent of 1228, and in the Lent of the following year. And it was here that he wrought a most striking miracle. During the funeral oration of a famous usurer, while he was developing the text, "Where thy treasure is, there is thy heart also", he suddenly broke off, and directed his congregation to go and open the dead man's treasures. The relatives did so, and, to their horror, found his heart still palpitating in the center of the heap of gold. This sobering prodigy did much to bring men to their senses, and helped toward reconciling the contending parties in Florence.

But Guelph and Ghibelline still strove for mastery. The former sought to destroy feudalism and build up commerce. The latter remained imperialists and reactionaries. In this strife, as in England in a similar case later, the nobles either were entirely wiped out or lost their power. Wealth began to dictate; money begot bankers.

The Albizzi, the Medici and like families rose into a power that lasted for generations, and subordinated the government of the cities of Italy to the might of gold. Heresy and hatred for the Church were woven into the struggle. With the tireless energy of an apostle, Saint Anthony went from city to city, calling on the leaders to make peace, preaching to the people of the life to come, exhorting all to abandon strife and to do penance. He preached in Rimini, he preached in the hamlets and in the hills. And one account of him shows the extraordinary extent of his missionary labors at this time.

"Anthony, ever faithful to his mission," says Father de Chérancé, "gave himself no truce in his combat with error, no repose in propagating the truth. On leaving Rimini he sailed along the shores of the Adriatic and landed on the coast of Illyria, giving missions through the maritime portions of the Gulf of Trieste from Aquileia to Venice, passing through Gorizia, Udine, Gemona and Conegliano. Here he attacked the Patarines in their last entrenchments, while at the same time he gathered in the degenerate Catholics who had lapsed into indifference.

"Thus ended the year 1227. With the spring of the year Anthony left Gemona, and passing through Treviso and Venice, joined his brethren at Padua. In all his journeys he seemed to be guided by an invisible hand, urged on by an interior voice which was ceaselessly re-

peating, 'Forward, forward, yet more souls to save.'
When he entered the walls of the ancient city, he was
overcome with an emotion partaking of fear and hope.
The element of hope, however, was predominant, though
the wonderful labors and glorious results in store for him
were as yet hidden from him."

Whether his footsteps led him to all these places
within this year we do not know; but we do know that,
in the designs of Providence, those feet that had traveled
so far were nearing the city which has claimed him since,
and has guarded his name and his fame with fierce
jealousy. Saint Anthony came to Padua probably in 1228.

14

Toward
the Journey's End

P ADUA, at the beginning of the thirteenth century, was a surprisingly wealthy city. If we
regard for a few moments the historical background we have blocked in, we shall understand why this was so, and also why a different type of
preaching was necessary here.

First and foremost, Padua was Guelphic, and we have
said that the pope's party was progressive, eager to found,
foster and develop commerce whenever possible. Standing in a fertile region, in a commanding position, with a
policy of commercial expansion and enterprise strong
within it, Padua developed crafts and guilds or what we
should call industries and unions, and concomitant wealth.
It founded its famous university in 1222.

The second factor which added wealth, genius and
prestige to Padua resulted from the circumstance, already
noted, that men looked to their own individual faction
for protection. Now we have said that the larger cities
were, so to call it, independently Guelphic or Ghibelline.
The result was that the smaller towns aligned themselves

with these more powerful neighbors, strengthening the latter while they themselves gained in security. The nobles, too, drew near to the cities; for a midnight raid might leave a castle in ashes and a family extinct. And so by force of circumstances, many of Italy's noblest families became citizens of Padua, bringing to her their wealth and their sophistication.

We come to the third factor. Virgil wrote plaintively in his ninth Eclogue: "Mantua, vae, miserae nimium vicina Cremonae!" (Mantua, alas, that is too near to unhappy Cremona!) It was not that the poet despised Cremona; but Cremona had been handed over to soldiers as the spoil of war; and since it was not large enough to make parcels for all, Mantua had been drawn on to supply the deficit. A paraphrase might be made of that line to describe the situation of Padua, who had for her neighbor Verona: "Padua, vae, miserae nimium vicina Veronae!" For as Padua was Guelphic, Verona of course must be Ghibelline, and they were at each other's throats after the fashion of the time. Both cities were wealthy, and both had strong governments. Padua had a podesta (mayor), assisted by sixteen city fathers and two city councils, a major and a minor. "The people," as one historian has said, "had a share in the government without however being able to impose upon it their blind wishes and thoughtless caprices."

The podesta of Verona at this time held his position by virtue of a compromise he had made with a raider known as Ezzelino III — a fierce Ghibelline who, by a sortie, had driven out the Guelphs from Verona and imposed his will on the city. We mention this here for we shall meet Ezzelino later in our story.

These three factors — commerce, wealth and border war — had brought about great looseness of life. While no heresy was to be encountered in Padua, preachers had to exert themselves to the utmost to keep in check the tide of immorality. The Paduans, though on the side of the pope politically, were hardly a choice example of the virtues that the Church inculcates and fosters. There was, in consequence, general rejoicing among the prelates, priests and respectable citizens at the news that Anthony, the great Franciscan preacher, was coming to draw his sword against the monster of licentiousness. Whether by accident or design, Anthony arrived in Padua just before Lent. The bishop begged him to give the Lenten course.

Holy Scripture shows us that while sins of the flesh are amongst the most abhorrent to God, as witness Sodom and Gomorrah, recovery from these sins can be very complete, as witness Mary Magdalen. It has often been noted that Christ treated such sinners with consideration while He publicly lashed hypocrites. And as it was in His life, so it continues; in the after years, some of His choicest graces were given to men and women who fell through human weakness and rose again through prayer and penance. Saint Augustine is precisely such a saint, and he is styled "Cor Ecclesiae", "The Heart of the Church"; while the Franciscan Order boasts of its Margaret of Cortona.

Padua, on Anthony's arrival, was in a sorry plight indeed. But faith remained: and while faith lives, the sinner needs only penance to make his soul fair and beautiful again, and to reclaim his body as a temple of the Holy Ghost. This is a comforting doctrine; for a sensual man who still has faith is being ground between two heavy stones, and something must happen. The grain of faith and the chaff of sensual pleasure will eventually become separated: the grain either to sprout into new life or die forever; the chaff to whirl "light before the wind" in the murky storms of the inferno.

Padua harkened to her preacher and was saved. Anthony told of God's love for the sinner in words of beauty never before heard by these pleasure-loving people. He painted the terrors of hell in colors not surpassed by Umbrian artists. From the very first, the churches wherein he spoke were crowded to suffocation. Soon he had to set up his pulpit out of doors. John Peckham gives this description of the city while Anthony preached:

"From all parts of the city and its neighboring villages people flocked in crowds to the sermons of the great

Franciscan. The law courts were closed, business was suspended and labor interrupted. All life and movement were concentrated at one point: the sermons and instructions of the mighty Wonder-worker. Soon the churches could not contain the audiences; he had to preach in the open air. The plant, dried up by the heat of the sun, thirsts for the dew of the early morn; more lively and impatient was the desire of the Paduans for the coming dawn and the hour for which the conferences were announced. From midnight the city was in motion. Knights and great ladies, preceded by lighted torches, pressed round the temporary pulpit; a motley multitude covered the plain, while the bishop, accompanied by his clergy, presided at the services. The numbers often reached thirty thousand. At the hour fixed Anthony would appear, in outward demeanor modest and recollected, his heart full of love. All eyes were fixed upon him, and when he began to speak, the crowds, hushed into silence, listened to his words with an immovable attention. At the conclusion of the discourse the enthusiasm of his hearers could not be contained; it burst forth in sobs, shouts of joy, or applause, according to its effect upon each listener. The crowd would rush upon the Saint. Everyone wished to see him closer, to kiss the hem of his habit or his crucifix; some even went so far as to cut bits of cloth from his habit to keep as relics. A bodyguard of young men kept near him, to prevent his being crushed by his admirers. For the most admirable effects he achieved were these: enmities were appeased and contending families publicly reconciled; usurers and thieves made restitution of their ill-gotten goods; great sinners struck their breasts in humble repentance; abandoned women fled from the haunts of vice and gave themselves up to penance. The confessionals were besieged, vice disappeared, virtue revived, and within the space of a month the aspect of the ancient city was transformed."

Where you have carrion you will have vultures, and where you have wealth and profligacy, you will have the money-lender. Padua, among other ailments, was suffering in her decaying members from usurers. And here we shall attempt to clear up, as well as our space allows, a certain confusion that produces criticism of the Church for condemning the practice of interest-taking. Let us recall that, when this condemnation was active, money was not used as a medium for making more money; that is to say, investments, in our sense of the term, were unknown. Money then was an inert commodity, for banks did not exist. Interest was ill-regulated and in the hands of lenders who sometimes charged the whole amount of the capital and over, for their loans. It was for the benefit of the poor and the foolish that the Church acted. As a matter of fact, the Franciscans of those days started what might be called a rudimentary banking system, in the interests of the poor, and for the protection of those who had money to lend. Since they themselves were bound by their stringent vow of poverty, and known to all as being incapable of taking any money for their part of the transaction, they were in a fit position to arrange loans between those who needed to borrow money, and honest rich men who could afford to lend it.

We must note, too, that in Padua not the least of Anthony's activities was interceding for the release from prison of men whom usurers had caused to be sent there, after having bled them white. The unjust steward in the Gospel is particularly contemptible in this, that while he was forgiven a debt that amounted to a fortune, he refused to forgive his fellow-servant a debt of a few dollars. The usurers of the thirteenth century were this man's brothers; for they actually and literally took men's whole fortunes by usury, and then had them thrown into prison "till they paid the last farthing."

The loan-office shark has always been a danger to imprudent plungers, and in his day, in Padua, our Saint took the first steps toward driving this shark to deeper water. For, thanks to Anthony's intervention, in 1231 Padua passed an ordinance to the effect that "no one could be kept in prison if he had yielded all his property to his debtors."

The chroniclers of the past wrote lives and histories after a method exactly the opposite of the one we are trying to follow. They record practically nothing but miracles, and then leave you quietly by yourself, with a box of colored wonders, to reconstruct from them the personality of him who produced them. The assumption is, apparently, that if you hear of one miracle you will be immediately granted another of your own, wherein you will see in vision the saint at work. We have endeavored in these chapters, somewhat nervously at times, to introduce the man first, and then reverently and intelligently to look on, so to speak, while he works the wonder; for we feel the observation to be deeply true that "we must meet the man to know the saint." The ancients who wrote the first legends and biographies introduce you to the saint first and to the humble and self-effacing man — usually — not at all.

Literally scores of miracles are related of Saint Anthony during this time in Padua. We will give only two.

A certain man of Padua called Leonard, in a quarrel with his mother, threw her down and kicked her. After this, the lout somehow or other got into a church where Anthony was preaching; and whatever emotion passed with him for sorrow entered his soul and drove him to confession. He told his sin. "The foot that could kick

a mother deserves to be cut off," said Anthony dryly.
Now Leonard, as might be expected from his filial activities, was not a man of native imagination or trained
sensitiveness to anything, including the finer figures of
speech. He plodded home, took a hatchet and cut off
his foot. By way of explanation for his rather peculiar
act, he said that Anthony had told him to do it. The
mother ran off to the church bitterly reviling the man who
had given such advice to her son. In a certain sense she
was right; Saint Anthony might have known that you
cannot use hyperbole with a person who kicks his mother
around the kitchen. But he heard her through and returned with her to the hut where Leonard was lying in a
pool of blood, looking surprisedly from the severed foot
that he held in one hand to the gory ax that he still
gripped in the other. Anthony took the foot, adjusted it
to the bleeding leg, made the Sign of the Cross over it,
and "the bones were knit together, the flesh held, and the
young man rose up quite sound, giving thanks to God
and the Franciscan Wonder-worker."

We shall take the account of the second miracle from
the *Legend of Saint Anthony* by Jean Rigauld, a Franciscan of Limousin whose work is dated approximately
1300:

"About the year 1292, a very old man told one of
the Friars that he had known Blessed Anthony. 'I was

a robber by profession,' he said, 'I belonged to a gang of a dozen brigands; we lived in the forest and plundered all the passers-by. But having heard the fame of Blessed Anthony's preaching, we resolved to go in disguise, the whole twelve of us, on a certain day to hear his sermon, for we could not believe all that was said about the power of his words. They compared him to a flaming torch and called him a second Elias. One evening, therefore, when he was to preach, we went to hear him, and no sooner had his burning words sounded in our ears than we began to feel bitter remorse and compunction for our sins and evil deeds. When the good Father had heard our confessions, one after another, and had given a suitable penance to each, he forbade us positively to return to our former life, promising to those who did so unspeakable sufferings. Some,' added the old man, 'resumed their criminal life, and very soon perished, as the Saint had foretold, by a most terrible death; but those who remained faithful slept in peace in the Lord. As for myself, the Saint had imposed on me the penance of going twelve times in pilgrimage to the tombs of the Apostles, and I am now on my way from Rome for the twelfth time.' This account was given to the Friar by the old man with many tears as they walked: he hoped for the joys of eternal life according to the Saint's promise, having abandoned the evil life he had once so miserably led."

At the beginning of this chapter we promised to return to Ezzelino. In the story of this man, told by many authors but told best, we think, by Alice Curtayne in *Assisi* (March, 1931), we shall note how the feuds of the Middle Ages ran from generation to generation, caused the extinction of families and brought misery to whole communities. We shall also see that if, through the years, Padua has been jealous of the honor of Anthony, Anthony has been no less jealous of the honor of Padua. For twenty-five years after the death of the Saint, during the octave of his feast, he came in his power to deliver the city that is so peculiarly his own.

We recall that the podesta of Verona, Padua's hostile neighbor, retained his office by treaty with the aristocratic plunderer Ezzelino. This man, whose family came to Italy with Emperor Conrad II, was the third of his line. Ezzelino I was "The Stammerer"; Ezzelino II was "The Monk"; Ezzelino III was "The Ferocious". Anthony's first contact with him resulted from his having taken many Guelphic prisoners at the time he threw in his lot with the Ghibellines in Verona. Anthony, as we know, intervened for men languishing in prison for debt. He also, in the interests of humanity, intervened for prisoners of war. He went to Ezzelino, therefore, on a mission of mercy for the hapless Guelph captives — and lost.

Later, to resume briefly, Ezzelino descended on the

fortress of one of the nobles of Padua — Tiso da Campo San Piero — and took prisoner his grandson Guglielmo. Padua rallied to her citizen, and marched off to rescue the child. Padua won. Then Ezzelino, with the aid of the people of Treviso, seized the Archbishop of Belluno's estates. The prelate, too, was a citizen of Padua. Once more the city marched against Ezzelino, fanning to fresh flames the insane hatred he had long felt against her.

Though the quotation is not short, we will let Alice Curtayne describe this cross-section of mediaeval history — a cross-section deeply grained with hate and blood:

"There is a picture in the Church of Santa Maria delle Grazie, Brescia, painted by Il Moretto, which depicts Saint Anthony of Padua in the act of rebuking Ezzelino III da Romano, a man immortal for infamy, whose tenure of the Signory of Padua is one of the blackest pages of Italian history. The picture shows the tyrant in a posture of meekness, as though quailing before the stern gesture of the Saint. History does not precisely bear out this representation. But it is a very interesting inquiry to find out exactly what measure of historical truth lies behind that scene, which seems to have pleased so greatly the fancy of Il Moretto.

"At the date of Anthony's embassy to him, Ezzelino was no worse than any of the contemporary petty warlords. He had not yet won for himself that evil repute

now inseparable from his name. All the Italian potentates of his kind were involved in feuds, vendettas that
were transmitted from father to son, so that a man would
inherit a mortal enmity toward a family, or toward a
group of families, and perhaps spend his life trying to
discount this perverted 'debt of honor'. But Ezzelino's
feud was distinct from all others in this, that he was
dedicated to vengeance on a whole community, the Re-
public of Padua. The strangest thing to be set down then
concerning this strange being, more monster than man,
is his mortal hatred for Padua: one man ferociously pitted
against a township. Padua was merely indifferent, or
scornful, toward her unpleasant neighbor until, by an
unexpected sequence of events, he became her sole ruler,
and then indeed she experienced the reality of that passion. It ground her to the extremest verge of annihi-
lation.

"What appears to be a horrible detail about the business is that this fury of vengeance was not Ezzelino's
personal affair. Padua had never given him any cause
for offense. He had inherited the rage from his father.
... Injured in the honor of his house by a Paduan nobleman, [he] had applied for justice to the Governors of
Padua. A certain punishment had been meted out to the
offender, but it was so inadequate in the eyes of the injured man that all Padua then became implicated in the

guilt, and his son was pledged to have revenge on Padua. The cause does not explain the effect, but the ways in which insanity lays hold on a man are legion. Long after his father's death, when the origin of the affair was becoming vague in the public mind, Ezzelino's hatred of the Paduans had mounted to a sort of insane obsession.

"We shall not weary the reader with the story of the devious petty victories through which this man became sole lord of Padua, six years after the death of Anthony. It is related that when Ezzelino rode into the hapless city, he backed his charger and grimly kissed the portals of the gate. That night there were speeches of welcome, bonfires, bell-ringing and music in the streets; but all the heads of the noble families, knowing their man, silently dispersed into exile under cover of darkness. . . .

"No one was immune, because he was bent on exterminating the Paduans. People were imprisoned for a look, for merely walking the streets with an air of freedom. Within a few months his dungeons were crowded, and executions and torturings in the public squares had become such a commonplace, they no longer drew spectators. . . .

"Among the legion of things he prohibited in Padua were preaching, confession and visits to churches. The people opposed a passive resistance to this mandate. With all their leaders in exile or killed, any organized reaction against the tyrant was impossible, but Ezzelino found that the smoldering fire of resistance was being kept alive by the Franciscans. He made an effort to exterminate them, as he had exterminated nearly all the chief families of Padua, but in the case of the Friars Minor, it was different. As fast as they were thrown into prison, their numbers were replenished from outside. Behind them stood an authority which Ezzelino could not reach, and beyond that authority again, there was the Church.

"And finally the Church thundered against Ezzelino. The Pope proclaimed a Crusade against him, precisely in the same terms as the war upon the Saracens. It must be unique in history, this case of a Crusade being proclaimed against a single man. All the Christian potentates of the peninsula were invited to support the army of the Papal Legate. . . .

"The siege of Padua is one of the great tales of history. The Legate exhorted the army on the morning the city was sighted, and chanted the *Vexilla regis prodeunt*. The rush of assault was made in a spirit of exaltation rather than of valor. Ezzelino's mercenaries, defending the walls, fought savagely. Recall the methods of that period: cannon were not used but huge battering-rams, which were driven against the walls by soldiers crouching under their shields, and movable towers were brought alongside, from which projectiles were hurled. The defense consisted mainly in throwing down boiling water,

burning pitch and oil, fire, rocks, sulphur, even salted
meat ignited. Behind this outer fringe of defense were
the lances and crossbows. 'So fearful was the noise,'
says the chronicler, 'it seemed as though the whole world
were crashing into ruin.' A tower that stood inside the
main gate of the city was set on fire, so that the defenders
were forced to yield a little, and immediately a breach
was effected in the walls, and the Legate's army poured
into the ctiy. They went to open the prisons, and in one
building alone they found fifteen hundred—men, women,
children, clergy, religious, all herded together in dark and
noisome dungeons. These formed a dreadful procession
as they emerged, shielding their eyes from the unaccus-
tomed daylight, which seared their eyeballs. They were
diseased and verminous, most of them idiotic, and many
came dragging skeletons of their dead along with them.
Ezzelino was not then in the city he had well-nigh ruined,
but he was captured later on in an engagement and died
shortly afterward, 'not of his wounds, but of rage.'

"One detail of that siege remained in the memory
of civilian onlookers. . . . Through the smoke of the
assault, they saw that it was a Friar Minor who was
directing the construction and movements of the batter-
ing-machines that were being pounded against the walls.
His voice could be heard above the racket, shouting and
directing, and he never left that zone of death, his face

streaming with the heat. And when the relief army poured through the breach, they noted that the first to scale the outer ladder and lead the soldiers through was another Friar Minor, companion to the first. The date was June 20, 1256, that is, within the octave of the Feast of Saint Anthony, to whom a novena for succor had been put up by all of the Faith within the city. If Moretto's picture does not represent an encounter in life, its symbolical truth is evident. When Ezzelino flouted Anthony's plea for mercy, he had by no means heard the last of the resolute Friar. Anthony, too, had a claim on Padua, which he vindicates even till this day."

15

The Close of the Day

NTHONY attended the General Chapter held in Assisi in May, 1230. It was on this occasion that he fell foul of Brother Elias—that dark shadow which passes through every chapter of the Franciscan history of this period. It is necessary for the sake of clarity to give some brief notice to this encounter; for in it we see Anthony, in the same spirit of fearlessness which had led him to rebuke an archbishop in the presence of his synod, and beard a brigand in the strength of his fortress, opposing one of the powers of his own Order on the steps of the Papal Throne.

When Saint Francis died, as we have seen, a basilica was built in Assisi under the supervision of Elias, for the remains of her most illustrious son. The church was finished in 1230; and it was decreed that when the Provincials gathered for the General Chapter, the body of Saint Francis should be transferred to the place of honor prepared for it. John Parenti was still Minister General, a position which Elias had wanted for himself. From this motive, presumably, Elias went to the city officials and persuaded them to take the body of Saint Francis from its present resting place in the Church of St. George, and transfer it to a secret chamber in the basilica. He alleged, as a reason, that some of the strangers in town were there only ostensibly to do honor to Saint Francis, and really to ascertain where his body was finally to be placed, so that later they might rob the city of this treasure.

The story was plausible, for citizens often went to war over the possession of saintly relics. Nor need we of today be too horrified at this; for in years recent enough to be called contemporary, Lincoln's body has been transferred more than thirty times, secretly, openly, and always in a clamor of bitter contention.

The city officials of Assisi did as Elias directed. But whatever he had in mind when he stole the body of the Patriarch of Assisi, the Papal Commission present for the translation, and all the assembled Friars, took it as an insult. They kept the affair a secret, however, so as not to cause a riot, and the solemnities of the translation were carried out in full.

Then followed the Chapter; and among the things to be considered was Elias' conduct in this case, and his attitude toward the Rule of the Order and the Testament of Saint Francis. There was apparently some strife in the Chapter regarding this last point, and Anthony, together with Adam Marsh, an Englishman, opposed Elias "to his

face" in Chapter, and later took the case to the Pope.
Gregory IX, on hearing the charge against Elias—namely,
that he wished to break down the stringency of the Rule
and encroach on Saint Francis' ideals of poverty — summoned before him all who had taken part in the Assisi
meeting. At the hearing Elias completely lost his head
and broke in on Anthony's testimony by calling out that
he was a liar. This interruption angered the Pontiff and
to that extent strengthened Anthony's case. It is said
that on this occasion Gregory IX offered Anthony the
purple, and again invited him to join the Papal Court.
If this actually happened, Anthony refused.

The case of Elias does not end here, but it is of no
more concern to us. We use it merely to illustrate another angle of Saint Anthony's character — devotion to
the Rule of the Order he had joined, respect for the ideals
of its founder, and an absolute fearlessness in the face
of opposition, whatever the consequences.

To return for a moment to the Chapter: the Minister
General, who had regarded Anthony with special favor
since his successful crusade against usury and luxury in
Florence, relieved him at the Assisi meeting of all cares
and offices of the Order, and gave him liberty to choose
residence in any house he wished. Pope Gregory ratified
this permission. Anthony chose St. Mary's, a Franciscan
Monastery in the city of Padua.

Some say that at this time he visited Mount La Verna. This may or may not be so; but he certainly was in Assisi: and we can picture the rapture which filled his soul as he trod again the rocks, the hillsides, the grassy paths, the very streets, so dear to the heart of Saint Francis. The trees whispered to Anthony of him whom they had often shaded as he sat and sang the Creator's praise in a voice that harmonized with all the music of nature. The birds hopped excitedly to the lower branches as Anthony approached, for he looked to them like their other brown-clad brother. The cliffs told him tales of Francis' penances and fasts; the flowers had heard of his tenderness and love. The sky above and the earth beneath; mountain peak and waterfall, the roads that lay in looped ribbons in the valley, the scalloped woods and the water-splashed rocks in the river — all spoke of the gentle heart that had pleaded for love in their midst; of the strong, winning face with its smile of encouragement for helpless things, its spontaneous pity for all hurt things, even the shyest, the lowliest, the most useless of God's creatures.

We know of only one thing strong enough to draw Anthony away from this sanctuary of memories: his zeal for souls. And before he left, he must have made a summary in his mind, as men do in the pauses that define the periods of living. Nearly ten years ago he had stood on the grass that grew around the Portiuncula, and gazed on Francis' face, before he himself departed for northern Italy. A lifetime of labor had crowded the decade since that day: preaching in Italy, preaching in France, and again in Italy; always the throng and the tumult; pleading and debating in the cities and the hamlets, working miracles in the hovels and in the hills; thousands of conversions, unnumbered confessions; discourses written, commentaries completed — such has been Anthony's life since he gazed on the face of the Poverello. Now Francis is gone, but his vast Order continues to grow. A great basilica stands on the hill and proclaims to the world the glory of him who ever fled from the world's notice and praise.

Anthony turned his steps from Assisi, as before, with the blessing of Saint Francis on his head; turned to northern Italy, to Padua standing rich and strong and expectant in the March of Treviso, waiting for her adopted son and most glorious citizen.

He arrived in the early autumn of 1230. Bishops, priests and people besought him to continue preaching, and he doubtless would have complied with their request had not the Cardinal of Ostia intervened. It was his desire that Anthony set down in writing "the results of his studies and experiences", and this work occupied the Saint's time for most of the winter. His *Sermons on the*

Feasts of the Saints are a result. He also established in Padua a retreat for sinners who wished to pass the remainder of their days in works of heroic penance.

Lent came — the season which had ever been a harvest time wherein this holy husbandman had gathered souls for heaven. Perhaps it was this which moved the Prince of Evil to attack him one night while he was asleep. Saint Anthony awoke to find that the devil had him by the throat, strangling him. He called to Mary, his Immaculate Mother, to save him; and at the very mention of her name, Satan fled.

But though Satan could do him no hurt, he was not exempt from another power. Spring, that brought new life to all things and filled the Romagna with song and gladness, only brought nearer to Anthony the threat of that mortality which, since Eden was shut, has spared neither sinner nor saint, not the very Author of life Himself. The Saint (by this time he was hailed as such) was not confined to bed, in spite of the fact that disease and the aggravations of toil and penance were slowly forcing him to the grave. He still was able to preach short sermons to the people, though with the approach of the summer months he was unwilling to detain them from their labors in the fields, or their commercial pursuits.

To the day of his death, he delighted in long walks through the woods and over the hills. While returning with a companion from one of these quiet rambles, he paused on an eminence overlooking Padua; and as Christ, toward the end of His life, had stood above Jerusalem and wept for the city He loved, as Francis had looked down on Assisi and blessed it with voice and hand, Anthony gazed on the gleaming turrets and noble walls of Padua, and foretold the future glories that the city was to know.

Feeling that death would soon claim him, he determined to spend as much time as possible in contemplation. With this in view, he approached a nobleman whose estate lay near Padua — in fact, that very Tiso da Campo San Piero whose grandson Ezzelino had carried off at an earlier date. Anthony asked that he and a few brethren be allowed to erect huts in the forest of the estate, that in the solitude of this place they might give themselves up to prayer and contemplation. Tiso gladly granted the request, and deemed it an honor to build Anthony's wattle hut with his own hands.

So in the stillness of the woods they raised a cell for Anthony — the last dwelling place of one who had been born in a palace. And he occupied it with gratitude, he who had given up his hereditary right to the Governorship of Lisbon. And he whose voice had swayed thousands in Milan and Toulouse; whose eloquence had driven proud Padua to her knees, and conquered royal

Rome itself; who might have ended his days in the Papal
Court "clothed in purple and falling lace" — elected to
wear till the end the brown habit of Francis and to live
in a home of wattles and rushes. His hut was beneath
"a walnut tree that rose high above the others, from the
stem of which sprang six branches in the form of a
crown." This was the only crown that the latest Bouillon
desired — a crown made of red wood, as his Master's
had been, though it was wrought by nature and Christ's
was fashioned by man.

In the year 1231, June 13 fell on Friday. At noon,
Saint Anthony came from his cell, as he had done even
in those distant days at Monte Paolo, to attend the common meal. A sudden weakness fell upon him, and his
companions supported him from the table. Knowing
that death had come, he said to the Brother at his side:
"If you approve of it I will go to Padua, to the Monastery
of St. Mary, to avoid trouble for the brethren here."

The brethren agreed — not to be rid of Anthony but
feeling that in the city he would receive better care in
his illness. None of them believed him about to die.
A cart was prepared to take him into Padua. The Friars
had two monasteries there: St. Mary's in the city proper,
and Arcella, on the forest road, close to the Convent of
the Poor Clares.

During that journey to the city Anthony grew steadily

weaker. The Brother with him, seeing this collapse and fearing that death might come before they reached St. Mary's, urged that they stop at the friary in the suburb of Capo di Ponte. This decision was to bear bitter fruit. Upon their arrival, Anthony confessed and received absolution; then in sinking strains the voice that had thrilled Europe for ten years intoned the hymn to the Blessed Virgin: *O Gloriosa Domina.* As the Saint lay on his cot he kept his eyes turned toward heaven. A Brother asked him what he saw; and with his face wearing a soft radiance even under the encroaching pallor of death, he replied: "I see my Saviour." The holy oil of unction was brought. "Brother," said he, to the priest preparing to anoint him, "there is no need for you to render me this service, for I have this unction within me. Nevertheless it is good, and gives me happiness." The words of the Penitential Psalms were the last that Saint Anthony uttered. As the sun sloped earthward, striking white gleams from the Alpine wastes upon the plains of Languedoc, this whiter soul took flight. He went along the wake of day, to meet his Saviour Who had come to take His cherished disciple home to the Tabor of eternal light.

16

Padua
Honors Her Saint

THERE was no cemetery attached to the Franciscan convent in the suburb where Anthony died, and he had left orders that his body be taken to the cemetery of St. Mary's in the city. The Friars, foreseeing only too well what would happen when an attempt was made to carry out this command, had done their best to keep his death a secret. But their caution was of no avail. The news leaked out; and the very children ran through the streets shouting, "He is dead, the holy father Saint Anthony is dead!" Hence, when the brethren from St. Mary's tried to remove the body from Capo di Ponte, the suburban populace, already informed, raised a terrific commotion. On the other hand, the people of the city were just as determined on their rights in this great matter.

The Friars appealed to the Bishop. He decided in favor of St. Mary's, and the podesta supported his decision. The only immediate effect being to increase the uproar, the podesta acted with determination. He summoned into a large assembly hall the faction from St.

Mary's vicinity, and simultaneously ordered the suburban-
ites to come into the city and remain there, under pain of
having their property confiscated. Then the Bishop, the
podesta, the city fathers, the city council, the clergy and
the Friars, went and brought to St. Mary's the body of
Anthony. The casket was borne on the shoulders of
Padua's leading citizens. All who were allowed to attend
— and crowds came from far and near — carried lighted
candles. And so, like a hero returning in triumph to his
native city, Saint Anthony entered Padua and took a new
possession of the hearts of all, that time has never relaxed
nor distance diminished.

His tomb immediately became a shrine. People from
every country in Europe came to be cured of their maladies; and the healthy brought the afflicted on stretchers.
Ills of the soul, too, were healed at his tomb. The priests
of St. Mary's were scarcely able to hear the confessions of
all the sinners who were drawn by the sweet and saving
influence of Anthony in death, even as others had been
drawn by him to grace during life.

He had already been canonized by popular acclaim,
as we have seen. The Paduans now petitioned the Pope
to make the honor official. Forty-seven duly attested miracles were presented to Gregory IX, and the Pope,
convinced of Anthony's sanctity, caused his name to be
written in the calendar of the Church (Spoleto, May 30,

1232). We read that, as the Supreme Pontiff declared Anthony a Saint, the bells of his native Lisbon pealed out of their own accord. Anthony had heard at Coimbra the voice of Francis coming to him in silver sweetness across the Alpine heights and down the valleys of Portugal, calling him to service in the lands beyond the mountains and seas. Anthony had answered it, and now the same invisible force again traveled those wastes and valleys and set the bells to ringing out his honor in the city of his birth.

Padua, like Assisi, built a basilica to the name and greatness of her Saint. It was completed in 1263, and is the international shrine of him whom countless millions, day by day, invoke in their need.

Our story is done. Someone has noted man's chagrin when he compares the finished book with what he had vowed to make it. We have picked our way as best we could through the sources we had at hand. Perhaps in some places we have unconsciously erred, in selecting among confused details; but we are not overmuch disturbed, if, in the main, we have made Saint Anthony better known, have caused his influence to be a little more intimately felt. If there are mistakes in this short work, they are ours. If there be any glory, that must go to God. If there be any merit, it belongs to Saint Anthony.

The time in which he lived is a puzzling page of history. The active work Anthony found himself undertaking in the new Franciscan Order, after he had been trained for a studious, quiet life among the Canons Regular of St. Augustine, must have tried to the utmost, at times, both his powers of adaptability and his faith in his new vocation.

Yet Saint Anthony's time and Saint Anthony's experience differ little in essence from our own, and the unexpected tasks in life that we are called on to undertake. The losses we must sustain, the sorrows we must endure, the bafflements and frustrations we must submit to, are also puzzles; and life itself is an impenetrable paradox, and will remain so to the end, unless read with the key given us by Christ Himself. He tells us that the seed must die to live; that the foolish are wise, and the wise foolish. This is the Gospel we must understand if we are to reach happiness. It is the Gospel that Anthony understood so well, knew by heart, made the basis of all his sermons and all his thoughts, and preached so sweetly and so convincingly to others. It is the Gospel that he preaches to us even in this distant day.

In life his was the task of serving others; in death it has not been different. In the Monastery at Coimbra, in the cave at Monte Paolo, before the tabernacle in prayer and in deep thought, he solved for himself the problem of a reversely written world; and having obtained the answer, he undertook to help others see the beautiful mystery. His task has been fruitful in happiness to men. The world has solicited him long for the sympathy, aid and love which it so earnestly craves and cannot find by itself. And as surely as the cry arises from earth, the answer comes from heaven.

Earth holds many sorrows which need divine wisdom to give them meaning. She has beauties and joys, but they are powerless against pain. Entrancing as are the sunsets that bronze the forest tops, they do not answer the question why the babe lies lifeless in its mother's arms. Soft and deep as is the pulse of a summer night, it fails to explain why a strong young man is caught in grinding wheels and mutilated for all the years to come. Moor and meadow are broad and peaceful, but they do not tell heart-broken parents why a child has returned love and sacrifice with an ingratitude that chills and darkens their age. When a man is overcome with pain he seeks a divine guide to a Divine Helper. When a man is in sin, he needs Divine forgiveness. Our guide will lead us to both.

What is called the wisdom of the saints is, in reality, to grasp clearly that sorrow is joy; that pain and hunger are blessings.

That is why we need Saint Anthony; for on earth all things read backward. Where others found perishable beauties, Anthony beheld the harmony of nature and faith. In all life he saw only one discordant note, and that was sin. He found good in even the most degraded of beings, and felt that this hidden spark might become a pure flame, since nothing is impossible to divine grace. He never despaired of the sinner, because of the superabundant mercy of God. He sanctified natural inclinations as reflections of God, united in a concert of praise, and he called upon every spirit to glorify the Lord. He inspired unbelievers to abandon their errors, and enemies to become reconciled. Through the zeal of Padua's Saint, wrongs were righted, virtue was revived and churches and public squares resounded with thanksgiving.

In this manner will Anthony lead us also to the beautiful mountains, by apparently turning us away from them. He will bring us to true riches, by teaching us to forget worldly gain; to true joy, by winning us from vain and harmful things. This young Saint who long ago, in a monastery garden, learned the beautiful key to life's enduring contradiction, will teach us who are ignorant, confirm us who are weak, and guide us all to that felicity whereof "it hath not entered into the heart of man to conceive", if we but ask it trustingly, in the name of Him Who was alike Anthony's Teacher and his Goal.

17

Devotion
to Saint Anthony

THE GIFT of speech is one of the great differentiating faculties that set man apart from all other orders of creation. The sky is mute in its beauty. The mountains give forth no articulate utterance of the calm and eternal strength they silently convey. The flowers lift our thoughts to Him Whose beauty and purity they dimly shadow; but no tongue within them speaks. Even the most enthralling songsters merely reëcho the melodies sung since the beginning of creation; while the brute creature still tells its wants in the same monotonous calls and lowings that have rung for a thousand generations through jungle and mountain pass.

Man has used his tongue to bless and to curse, to soothe and to hurt, to bestow and to deny. It is a critical faculty, in the sense that a great part of man's salvation hangs directly on it — as Saint James noted when he declared, under inspiration, that he who did not offend with his tongue was a perfect man. There have been many tongues on earth worthy of eternal remembrance for the messages they delivered to fellow-mortals. But one tongue alone did God Himself select to remain alive through the centuries, the symbol of perpetual blessing and pleading — and that was the tongue of Saint Anthony of Padua. The mortal frame of Padua's Saint moldered into dust, but his tongue God preserved as an assurance to us all that Saint Anthony is still our eloquent advocate, our ready helper.

Nor has that symbol been misleading; for in all the casual daily needs of men's and women's lives, in all the little trials that the hours count out to us, in all the cares of our workaday activities, Saint Anthony has consistently and successfully interested himself. And simply because he has been man's constant advocate and helper, man in turn has shown him continual reverence. More homage has developed for this Saint than for any other figure that we can descry on history's pages. The aim of this chapter is to set forth some of the devotions that are so many bouquets on the shrine of his greatness.

THE MIRACULOUS RESPONSORY

One of the first of these devotions is known as the Miraculous Responsory. It was probably composed by Julian of Speyer, a contemporary of the Saint, who died about 1250, and who wrote the ancient liturgical offices for the feasts of Saint Francis, Saint Dominic and Saint

Anthony. Each strophe enumerates miracles performed by the Saint. But if Julian of Speyer wrote it, it was Saint Bonaventure who, as Minister General, gave it prominence and publicity. The occasion was the finding of the incorrupt tongue of the Saint.

We have noted that the Basilica of Saint Anthony was completed in 1263. The city fathers and the clergy, major and minor, came to Padua to be present at the translation of the Saint's relics, and Saint Bonaventure traveled from Rome to preside. When the tomb was opened it was found that the flesh had crumbled to dust but that the tongue was intact, and had the appearance of the tongue of a living man. It was at sight of this that Saint Bonaventure gave utterance first to what is now universally known as the Antiphon of Saint Bonaventure, following which he intoned the Miraculous Responsory. We give both here:

Antiphon

O blessed tongue! that never ceased to praise God, and taught others to bless Him, it is now manifest how precious thou art in His sight!

V. Blessed Anthony, powerful preacher, pray for us.

R. That by thy intercession we may enjoy life eternal.

Responsory

If then you ask for miracles,
Death, error, all calamities,
The leprosy and demons fly,
And health succeeds infirmities.

The sea obeys and fetters break,
And lifeless limbs thou dost restore,
While treasures lost are found again
When young and old thine aid implore.

All dangers vanish at thy prayer,
And direst need doth quickly flee.
Let those who know thy power proclaim,
Let Paduans say — these are of thee.

The sea obeys and fetters break, etc.

To the Father, Son, all glory be,
And Holy Ghost eternally.

The sea obeys and fetters break, etc.

The Responsory gives a list, as we see, of the various
evils of the Middle Ages that afflicted and terrified mankind. And since many of the same evils are still with us

under the same or different names, this famous invocation is sung on Tuesdays during the devotions in honor of Saint Anthony in Franciscan churches. It is a very widespread and popular form of devotion to the Saint, a consolation to innumerable souls in their troubles, and a sure means of obtaining relief when used with faith and confidence.

THE TUESDAYS OF SAINT ANTHONY

The second devotion to Saint Anthony that we wish to mention, "Making the Tuesdays" in his honor, dates back to his funeral, Tuesday, June 17, 1231. The occasion was marked by so many and such astounding miracles that it still remains a unique date in history. Such a profound impression was made on all that on the successive Tuesdays afterward the people of Padua gathered in the churches to honor their Saint. Miracles continued on these occasions, and the custom became wide-spread. But since all things, devotions included, have their seasons, this practice by degrees fell into disuse. It pleased Saint Anthony himself to renew it.

"In the year 1616 there lived at Bologna a noble and pious couple, who after twenty-two years of married life were childless. One day the lonely wife, kneeling before the altar of Saint Anthony in the Franciscan church, laid before the Saint the sorrow of her life and begged his intercession. And lo! the Saint himself appeared before her and bade her visit his altar and pray before it on nine consecutive Tuesdays. This she did, and in course of time became a mother. But to the bitter disappointment of the parents, the infant was found to be horribly deformed. This new sorrow, however, proved to be but a further trial of their faith. The mother brought the babe to the altar of the Saint, and on touching it to the stone, all trace of deformity immediately disappeared. The fame of this prodigy, which the grateful parents spread everywhere, had the effect of reviving and popularizing the devotion of the Nine Tuesdays in honor of Saint Anthony.

"In the course of time the number of Tuesdays was raised to thirteen, in memory of the date of the death of the Saint (June 13). Pope Leo XIII richly indulgenced the devotion of the Thirteen Tuesdays" (*Franciscan Almanac,* 1931).

SAINT ANTHONY'S BREAD

Most of us are acquainted with the charitable devotion known as "Saint Anthony's Bread"; in a score of churches we have seen boxes set out in which the faithful may drop small alms to go to feed the poor who have recourse to this Franciscan "Table of the Lord". And if we have visited Europe or the British Isles and have been near a Franciscan house in the early afternoon, we have seen old men and women standing at the front doors of these houses waiting for this morsel of charity. At the appointed hour a young lay Brother, dressed in the identical garb of Saint Francis, and not unlike statues of Saint Anthony himself, opens the heavy door and hands out to the waiting line the loaves that the devotees of Saint Anthony have provided. In America, Franciscan houses carry out the same practice conformably with modern conditions.

This devotion goes back to primitive days and, like the other devotions, to Padua. Characteristically, it had its origin in a miracle: "A child two years old, whose parents lived in the vicinity of the basilica, then in course of erection, fell into a vessel of water and was drowned. After her first passionate outburst of grief, the mother had recourse to the Wonder-worker and Patron of the town, promising that if her prayer were heard she would give a measure of grain to the poor. Toward midnight, while the bereaved woman was still praying, the child rose up as if from sleep. This miracle gave rise to the practice of promising alms to the poor in return for favors received through the intercession of the Saint" (*Franciscan Almanac*, 1931).

Though this devotion survived the years, in the nineteenth century it received an impetus that started it on a course of greater power. There lived at Toulon, in France, a girl named Louise Bouffier. It was her intention and desire to become a nun, but circumstances made it necessary for her to provide for her parents. She tried her best to satisfy both her callings by remaining at home to work, and by devoting all her spare time to gathering prayers and alms for the Foreign Missions.

Louise kept a small store; and on arriving there one morning, found that she could not open it. A locksmith was called, but his professional skill proved equally useless. Do what he would, the lock held firm. In the manner of a general who is not confined to one line of attack, the locksmith decided to break down the door with a crowbar; but since he had not included this tool in his kit, it behooved him to return to his smithy. While he was away, poor Louise remained on the street in the center of the early morning crowd that had stopped to watch. It occurred to her to pray to Saint Anthony. She promised — as many before and since have done in some predicament — that if the Saint would help her get the door open without breaking it, she would give bread to the poor.

The locksmith came up with the crowbar. "I have promised Saint Anthony," Louise told him, "some bread for the poor. Try the key once more; the Saint will surely come to our aid." The man obeyed: the lock clicked open.

This was a trifling incident, but it warmed Louise's devotion to Saint Anthony, so that when, later, a girl gave her a small statue of him, she set it up in a little room at the back of the store, and placed two boxes before it. People who came for goods would drop into the room and put a few pennies into one box and a petition into the other. As the prayers were answered, these same people returned and brought their friends. The alms always went to buy food for the poor. It was thus that the room in the rear of Louise's store became a shrine at which petitions were granted, and suffering and want were relieved.

Louise died on April 7, 1908. The store was then closed; but this devotion had received a new stimulus, for her little statue and poor boxes were the forerunners of those that we see daily in our churches.

Saint Anthony's Brief

This devotion also goes back to the thirteenth century. The earliest documents give a detailed account of the miracle which began it. Father Roger Maloney, O. F. M., whose article in the *Franciscan Almanac* we have followed practically verbatim here, recounts it in this way:

"A certain woman of Lisbon frequently suffered from dreadful convulsions which seemed to indicate demoniacal possession. One day her husband, taunting her with her affliction, attributed it to guilt, whereupon the unfortunate creature was so cruelly upset that she determined to put an end to her life by drowning herself in the Tagus. While on her way to carry out her terrible resolution she passed a church of the Friars Minor. She bethought herself that it was the feast of Saint Anthony, and it occurred to her to enter to say a last prayer. While praying she fell into a kind of trance. She seemed to see the Saint standing near her, gazing at her gravely and compassionately, and holding in his hands a piece of parchment. This he gave to her, with the words: 'Arise, woman, and take this paper, which will free you from the molestations of the Evil One.' On coming to herself she was amazed to find in her hands the parchment. It bore these words from the Book of the Apocalypse (v, 5): 'Ecce Crucem Domini; fugite partes adversae! Vicit Leo de tribu Judae, Radix David, Alleluia, Alleluia!' (Behold the Cross of the Lord; fly, all hostile powers! The Lion of the Tribe of Juda, Root of David, hath conquered, Alleluia, Alleluia!) Calm and hopeful, the woman returned home, and from that day forward, as long as she kept the precious document in her possession, she was never troubled by the demon.

"Now it happened that the husband, in his gratitude for the favor received, published it everywhere. The story came to the ears of the King of Portugal. He had the woman brought before him, and was so impressed that he induced her to give him the parchment. The result was that the woman again became subject to her old affliction. In great distress the husband appealed to the Friars Minor to intercede with the monarch for the restoration of the precious document. They did so, but succeeded in obtaining only a copy, which, however, was found to have the same efficacy as the original. The name Brief (Latin: *Breve*) arose, according to some, from the concise phraseology of the document, but it is more probably due to the fact that in mediaeval times this term was applied to all documents of importance. The Franciscans, seeing the efficacy of the Brief, propagated its use, exhorting the faithful to keep it on their persons as a protection against all dangers, and particularly against the assaults of the Evil One. It soon became known and venerated in all Catholic countries."

Father Roger then cites a striking incident that proves further the power of this devotion; and adds some interesting and authenticated cases that show Saint Anthony's loving, personal concern for those who invoke his aid:

"In the winter of 1708 a vessel of the French navy was surprised by a terrific storm off the coast of Brittany. When things seemed hopeless, the chaplain, in the name of the whole crew, had recourse to Saint Anthony. He wrote on a piece of paper the words of the Brief and cast

it into the sea, with the invocation: 'O great Saint Anthony, hear our prayers.' Immediately there came on
winds and sea a great calm, and the vessel was enabled
to get safely to port. On landing, the crew betook themselves to a church to give public thanks for their rescue,
and as a further proof of their gratitude, they had a full
account of the miraculous event published in a newspaper
of the period (*Mercure Galant,* January, 1709).

"In connection with devotion to Saint Anthony, special
mention must be made of his well-known traditional
'Privilege' of finding lost things. We find an allusion to
it in one of the strophes of the famous Responsory:
'Membra, resque perditas,' etc. (Treasures lost are found
again, etc.), which proves that it dates from the Saint's
own time. In the sixteenth century the celebrated Franciscan, Pelbart of Temesvar, wrote: 'Just as during life the
Lord glorified Saint Anthony by giving him the grace of
bringing back straying souls, so now after his death He
gives him the power of restoring lost things to his clients.'
Later, a doctor of the University of Paris, William Pepin,
is more emphatic on the point: 'As I have often proved
by experience, Saint Anthony has received from God the
privilege of restoring lost things. And therefore I may
justly apply to him what Saint Bernard said of the Blessed
Virgin: "Let those deny their praise who can say that,
having implored thy help, they have not been heard!" '

The learned Bollandists who record these testimonies, in concluding their study of the wonder-working power of the Saint, declare: 'Everyone knows that Saint Anthony has been destined by God to restore to their rightful owners things lost or stolen.'

"In the records of the work initiated by Louise Bouffier we find innumerable cases. We shall cite but one. A lady found that bank notes to the amount of 1,400 francs were missing from her desk. She began a novena to Saint Anthony, promising that if the money were recovered she would give a generous donation to the poor. On the last day of the novena, while walking in her garden, she stumbled against a small package. Upon opening it, she discovered, to her surprise and joy, that it contained her money, with the exception of 200 francs. Later a servant came to her, confessing the theft. The servant declared that during the nine preceding days she had suffered grievously from the pangs of remorse; that morning, after a sleepless night, she had made up her mind to restore the money, but afterward, losing courage, she had placed it in the garden where the lady was accustomed to walk. She further confessed that she had already spent the 200 francs, but promised to restore them.

"From Rome comes a well-attested recent case. A little boy only three years of age, eluding the vigilance of his attendant, became lost in the streets of the city.

The distracted attendant and parents prayed earnestly to Saint Anthony. Soon afterward, the lad returned alone as if nothing had happened. He told how a Friar had conducted him in silence to the door, had rung the bell, and then departed."

S. A. G.

The letters "S. A. G." stand for the words "Saint Anthony Guide." They are of especial interest to us here, inasmuch as in January, 1924, the devotion which gave them prominence in the eighteenth century rose again in a new growth that has spread throughout the world.

We will first give an account of the miracle through which Saint Anthony became the special Patron of written messages and the Protector who watches over the safe delivery of our letters. Then we will mention briefly the organization that in recent years has done so much to spread this and other devotions in honor of Saint Anthony, namely, SAINT ANTHONY'S GUILD, of Paterson, New Jersey.

Here is the miracle. A certain merchant left Spain for Peru. Although his wife wrote several letters to him, she never received a reply. Finally she invoked Saint Anthony's aid With childlike confidence she went to the Franciscan church in Oviedo where she placed a letter in the hands of a statue of the Saint, begging him to deliver it to her husband. Later she returned to the church and to her great joy found, in place of her letter, a reply from her husband, together with several gold pieces. The letter, which may still be seen at Oviedo, is dated Lima, July 23, 1729, and states that the wife's missive was delivered by a Franciscan Father.

From this grew the laudable custom of writing S. A. G. on letters and of sealing letters with Saint Anthony Guide seals.

SAINT ANTHONY'S GUILD

In January, 1924, SAINT ANTHONY'S GUILD, under the guidance of the Franciscan Fathers of the Province of the Most Holy Name, and with Father John Forest, O. F. M., as Director, was founded. Its growth has been little less astounding than any of the other miracles that the Saint has performed. The Guild's first objective was to renew and spread the devotion to Saint Anthony that is indicated by the symbol, S. A. G. This met with such phenomenal success that the Guild felt encouraged to attempt other projects. In 1925 the first copy of THE ANTHONIAN was printed. This beautiful quarterly was kindly received by the public, as is evidenced by the innumerable letters that are sent to the Editor's office in its praise by readers in the most widely different stations of life. THE ANTHONIAN has been the occasion, likewise, of many beautiful and devotion-inspiring paintings by the great religious artist, C. Bosseron Chambers.

And behind all the Guild's varied and far-reaching activity is a purpose, a motive, one of the highest it is in man's power to pursue, one dear to the heart of Christ, His Church, Saint Anthony and the whole Franciscan Family. All that is done by the Guild, all the money that is earned, goes to the educating of boys for the sacred priesthood. Christ was a Teacher, and He formed a school wherein He trained His priests, His Apostles. Saint Anthony was a teacher, the first in his Order; and it is to the carrying on of his work that Saint Anthony's Guild is dedicated. Its success has been literally miraculous: a clear sign from heaven that the blessing of God and His servant Anthony is upon this work, which seeks no other end than to further the Kingdom of Christ and to honor Padua's glorious Saint.

Daughters of St. Paul

MASSACHUSETTS
50 St. Paul's Ave., Jamaica Plain, Boston, MA 02130; **617-522-8911**.
172 Tremont Street, Boston, MA 02111; **617-426-5464; 617-426-4230**.
NEW YORK
78 Fort Place, Staten Island, NY 10301; **212-447-5071; 212-447-5086**.
59 East 43rd Street, New York, NY 10017; **212-986-7580**.
625 East 187th Street, Bronx, NY 10458; **212-584-0440**.
525 Main Street, Buffalo, NY 14203; **716-847-6044**.
NEW JERSEY
Hudson Mall—Route 440 and Communipaw Ave.,
    Jersey City, NJ 07304; **201-433-7740**.
CONNECTICUT
202 Fairfield Ave., Bridgeport, CT 06604; **203-335-9913**.
OHIO
2105 Ontario Street (at Prospect Ave.), Cleveland, OH 44115;
    216-621-9427.
616 Walnut Street, Cincinnati, OH 45202; **513-721-4838; 513-421-5733**.
PENNSYLVANIA
1719 Chestnut Street, Philadelphia, PA 19103; **215-568-2638;**
    215-864-0991
VIRGINIA
1025 King Street, Alexandria, VA 22314; **703-683-1741; 703-549-3806**.
SOUTH CAROLINA
243 King Street, Charleston, SC 29401.
FLORIDA
2700 Biscayne Blvd., Miami, FL 33137; **305-573-1618; 305-573-1624**.
LOUISIANA
4403 Veterans Memorial Blvd., Metairie, LA 70006; **504-887-7631;**
    504-887-0113.
423 Main Street, Baton Rouge, LA 70802; **504-343-4057; 504-381-9485**.
MISSOURI
1001 Pine Street (at North 10th), St. Louis, MO 63101; **314-621-0346;**
    314-231-1034.
ILLINOIS
172 North Michigan Ave., Chicago, IL 60601; **312-346-4228; 312-346-3240**.
TEXAS
114 Main Plaza, San Antonio, TX 78205; **512-224-8101; 512-224-0938**.
CALIFORNIA
1570 Fifth Ave., San Diego, CA 92101; **619-232-1442**.
46 Geary Street, San Francisco, CA 94108; **415-781-5180**.
WASHINGTON
2301 Second Ave., Seattle, WA 98121; **206-623-1320**
HAWAII
1143 Bishop Street, Honolulu, HI 96813; **808-521-2731**.
ALASKA
750 West 5th Ave., Anchorage, AK 99501; **907-272-8183**.

CANADA
3022 Dufferin Street, Toronto 395, Ontario, Canada.